SPIRIT EYES

SPIRIT EYES

Uncovering God's Hidden Messages for You

Dan Lacine

SPIRIT EYES:
Uncovering God's Hidden Messages for You.
© Copyright 2021- Dan Lacine

Published by Adventures in Daily Living

All rights reserved. This book is protected by the copyright laws of the United States of America. No part of this book may be reproduced or used in any manner without the prior written permission of the copyright owner, except for the use of brief quotations in a book review or for a private study group. Scripture quotations marked NKJV are taken from the New King James Version. Copyright © 1982 by Thomas Nelson, Inc. Used by permission. All rights reserved. Scripture quotations marked TLB are taken from The Living Bible; Tyndale House © 1997, ©1971 Tyndale House Publishers, Inc. Used by permission. All rights reserved. Scripture quotations marked NLT are taken from the New Living Translation; © 1996, 2004, 2015 by Tyndale House. Used by permission. All rights reserved. Scripture quotations marked (NIV) are taken from the Holy Bible, New International Version, NIV®. Copyright © 1973, 1978, 1984 by Biblica, Inc. Used by permission of Zondervan. All rights reserved.
Cover image courtesy of Jozef Klopacka, Standard licensed obtained from 123RF.com.

ISBN: 978-1-7368257-0-9

Dedication

I dedicate this book to my wife, Betty, who has supported me during the entire process, from concept to writing to editing, formatting and publishing

Acknowledgments

I want to thank Morgan Gist MacDonald of Paper Raven Books, without whom I would never have completed this work. Thanks also to David Sluka who was my first mentor, starting me on the author journey through his writer's workshops. I am deeply indebted to my editors, Margaret Nelson and Lisa Newkirk who invested much time and effort to correct and improve the content and confirm the accuracy of names of places especially those that had changed. I appreciate the work of my beta readers: Lauren Allen, Linda Seals, Sherry Litz, Tulia Lacine, Diana Gray, and Julie Moenck. Finally, I thank those who first inspired me to take this journey when attending a Global Legacy leaders and pastors conference in 2014. One of the gentlemen in our prophetic group declared "Dan, I think there's a book in you."

Dedication	v
Acknowledgments	vii
Chapter Previews	xi
Introduction	13
1 The World Behind the Natural	19
2 Nature: What Can a Storm Tell You?	25
3 Art: Can a Painting Leave You Breathless?	37
4 Signs: Finding Direction When You're Lost	47
5 Music: How Does the Melody Move You?	55
6 Video: Hidden Messages Revealed	63
7 Movies: Messages That Influence Your Beliefs	73
8 Shopping: What's Right in Front of Your Eyes?	81
9 Sports: Pictures Seen 'Round the World'	87
10 Numbers and Secret Codes	95
11 Dream Language: Where the Spirit Reveals	103
12 Go Exploring	111

Chapter Previews

The World Behind the Natural
Once you see the natural world as a shadow of the spiritual, you will uncover purpose in what is happening. How do you develop the skill to see deeper?

Nature
The wonders of nature reveal a God of awesome beauty and variety. If you develop eyes to see, you will find God's messages here.

Art
Artists may portray pictures of God, angels, and heaven. Has a piece of art struck you with awe yet had no obvious spiritual content? Why do tears fill your eyes when gazing at one painting but another one bores you?

Signs
Storefront signs, highway signs, and billboards are placed to grab your attention. Discover significance in these examples: Welcome, North Carolina; WhyNaught Road; Liberty, Missouri. What deeper sense can you extract from these names?

Music
Lyrics in music are often self-explanatory, but the melody affects our emotions. What makes one song produce tears but another entices you to stand up and dance? Certain music triggers a connection from your souls to a God who loves you. How do you respond when you feel the spirit behind the music?

Video
From video games to YouTube, we are not bereft of eye-appealing visual entertainment. Can you find hidden messages in the world of entertainment? Music video clips bring vocalists' songs to life and enable them to share their vision with an on-demand audience.

Movies
Superhero movies are popular. Often the hero in the movie may not survive until the end -- or he or she may die and come back to life. Most movies have a message that parallels the good news that someone was willing to sacrifice his/her life to save another.

Shopping
Does God leave messages for you in plain sight? If you delve into the not-so-common titles of board games, cereals, and health foods, you will find values beyond what you expected.

Sports
From events during a Super Bowl to the names of teams and nicknames of players, there are many opportunities to capture messages that speak to you personally.

Numbers
Have you woken up at night to notice your alarm clock displaying 3:33, 12:21, or some other unique combination? Once you learn the meaning of some basic numbers, you will be able to translate God's messages to you.

Dream Language – God's favorite?
Dreams are called night parables. Jesus often told stories in parable form. At night, your spirit is open to thoughts and mental images from God. With your body at rest and your brain disengaged from active thought, it's a perfect time for your spiritual Companion to slip you messages. You can learn to unpack the picture language of dreams when you partner with the Spirit and practice thinking symbolically.

Introduction

The spiritual did not come first, but the natural, and after that the spiritual. 1 Cor 15:46.

I was playing hide-and-seek inside the house. I scoured every corner, peeked behind every couch, and scavenged through the hanging clothes in the closet. I still hadn't found my younger brother, Mark. I had exhausted every possibility. Had he moved into another room while I was looking in this bedroom? I searched again, checking the bathtub, opening the doors of the vanity, and finally gave up. He strode out of the blue bedroom where I had just finished searching!

"Where were you hiding?" I questioned, anxious to know.

"In the closet."

"No way! I just looked there and didn't see you."

He replied, "Did you check under the clothes pile in the corner?"

I had missed finding him, even though he was right in front of me! When I scanned the closet, I had expected to see a leg sticking out of the hanging clothes or a head bobbing up from behind the shelves. My expectations prevented me from noticing the large pile of clothes in the corner with a large lump. In the same way, our expectations prevent us from seeing into the spirit realm that exists all around us.

Have you missed a turn while driving because the route you take to work is so ingrained in your mind that you were on autopilot? I've done that - more than once. When we focus on the task at hand, we fail to "stop and smell the roses."

We are programmed to move from task to task that we don't allow our minds to wander -- or better still -- to wonder. By hurrying, we miss much of the beauty in the world around us. We can train ourselves to slow down and open the gate to allow our imagination to run loose. Imagination unleashes creativity. Creativity expands our minds to sense more than what is right in front of us.

The challenge is that we rarely allow ourselves to rest for a moment during our busy lives. Instead, we exhaust ourselves with the constant "Go-Go-Go." Music plays at every restaurant, not to mention the video screens screaming for our attention. Songs and commercials blare at gas stations too. The non-stop noise pervades the environment whether we step inside to grab a drink or stay outside to squeegee the windshield.

How can we escape the clamor? Rest seems elusive.

Creativity thrives in quiet places where rest calms our minds and our spirits are open to receive. In these places, we discover the inspiration that allows us to "see" into the invisible world around us using our "Spirit Eyes." I call this world the spiritual world.

First comes the natural, then the spiritual. The natural world, where we interact day in and day out, is not all that exists.

Introduction

God is always communicating

Good friends love to communicate and share with you. How does a good friend relate to you? A good friend likes to connect with you often: face-to-face, on the phone, via text, on Facebook messenger, and in other ways. You can't get enough of being with him/her. A good friend knows what you like, wants to be near you all the time, enjoys being with you without having to converse. He or she may bring you gifts, make you laugh, or do silly things to impress you as well as share day-to-day experiences. If God is personal, as this book assumes, why wouldn't He want to share His life with you in a like manner? For example, wouldn't He want to talk to you often - almost all the time? Wouldn't He want to be close to you and share everyday experiences? He would share experiences that are unique to your friendship. How near is God to you? Is he close-by like a friend, or do you picture Him up in the sky, far away?

How I started looking beyond the natural

Relaxing in our hotel room while attending a Christian Charismatic conference in Florida, my roommate switched on the TV. Cindy Jacobs, a recognized leader in prophetic circles, was speaking about supernatural realities. "First comes the natural, then the spiritual," popped out of her dialog and stuck in my mind.

Just a few hours earlier at breakfast, I had been chatting with a woman named Brenda, who was staying at the same hotel. I learned that Brenda had been mentored by Bob Jones in the prophetic (sensing God's impressions). Bob, who passed away in 2014, was regarded as a modern-day prophet by many charismatic Christians.

I asked Brenda to pray for me. I wanted her to impart that same insight and prophetic gift that she possessed.

Perhaps it was her prayer that morning that awakened my spirit to see far deeper than I had ever experienced before. This impartation impacted me significantly. I started viewing the world around me with new eyes - beyond the surface. I recognized a parallel between what I saw in the visible world and its symbolic meaning in the spiritual realm. This symbolic thinking reminded me of the difficulty I encountered as a college freshman.

In my literature class at Elmhurst College, the professor expected us to appreciate the symbolism in the classics. Symbolism - what's that? Though it was obvious to the professor, I had problems recognizing the symbolism in the books we read. I could see the literal pictures, but nothing more. What would you expect from a Math/Science major like me? In the scientific disciplines, you observe the world exactly as it looks on the outside.

I didn't see it then. But after praying with Brenda, I began to see the world with new eyes – Spirit Eyes. I was no longer observing only the external objects. It was like the scene in the original "Wizard of Oz" when Dorothy opened the door of the black and white farmhouse and stepped into the Technicolor Land of Oz.

Suddenly I yearned to dig for further meaning in *everything* I saw. I discovered that the world around me is a reflection of an invisible dimension where similar events occur. Through practice, I have been able to "see" the spiritual world behind the natural. I believe you can learn to see this way too.

I know that many others share my desire to find a deeper meaning in life. The purpose of this book is to help you develop the habits of expectancy and observation so that you can experience life in a new dimension.

Introduction

Learning to see "beyond the obvious" is the first step in finding God's hidden messages for you. A new world opens when you learn to observe with expectancy. That habit turns ordinary life into a daily adventure. Expect to unearth more meaning in what you're observing.

Come with me on a journey to discover the spiritual world around you. My hope is that you will begin to perceive the world in a deeper way that will change your normal routine into a daily adventure with the One who made you!

1 The World Behind the Natural

Once you see the natural world as a shadow of the spiritual, you will uncover purpose in what is happening. How do you develop the skill to see deeper?

You must believe three things to begin viewing the world with more purpose:

1. God is always communicating – not only through nature but in many other ways.
2. There is no such thing as a coincidence. Every incident has a purpose.
3. You can find meaning in a small event if you train yourself.

Practice searching for hidden messages. Interpret the clues as love messages from a Friend. When you expect God to speak to you in the events of your day, it will excite you and open your eyes to a new adventure.

Follow the examples and suggestions in the Exercises section of each chapter to get you started on this adventure. NOTE: You need not read these chapters in order. I recommend you finish this chapter and the nature chapter. You can select your favorites after that.

There is no such thing as a coincidence

The Hebrew language has no word for coincidence. Hebrew thought is that every event and every occurrence reflect God's guidance in our lives. Recently, Johnny a friend from church, shared this experience. Johnny has a couple of brothers. A tornado touched down, a mere 150 feet from his brother Gwen's house. The wind ripped through the field and raced ahead toward his second brother's house. The tornado closed in. Right in front of the house, the swirling wind lifted off the ground, crossed over the roof without incident, and then dropped down and continued rushing away leaving destruction in its path. Some would call that a coincidence. I call it a miracle.

Here's another instance of God's care: Upon leaving my house, I maneuvered through the curvy neighborhood streets, then down a steep hill to cross County Highway 11, which is a 50-mph highway where cars speed down a long hill. I spot cars here only occasionally. I paused at the stop sign and started crossing the highway when suddenly I hit the brakes, not knowing why. From out of nowhere a grey car streaked by right in front of me.! My heart pounded in my chest. My jaw dropped and I stopped breathing for a moment. When I realized I missed a crash, I exhaled a sigh of relief. I had not seen that car a second earlier. I avoided a T-bone collision! What made me hit the brakes without thinking? It was like instinct. God was watching over me.

The World Behind the Natural

I experienced another close call one fall day a few years ago. I was on my way to my duplex which is on a busy four-lane road. I braked to turn left into my driveway. As I was waiting for a break in the traffic, I glanced in the rear-view mirror in time to see a black car rapidly filling the view. BOOM! I felt a kick in my back. The dashboard lights went blank as a black Honda Accord crashed into my car and tore off the left quarter panel of my bronze Buick Riviera. My eyes popped open wide in surprise as the shock sunk in. A tingling sensation was climbing up my spine as I thought "This can't be happening to me. I have to be dreaming, but I'm not." I was sad that what had been my mom's car was now damaged. It was mid-afternoon, and the driver of the vehicle that hit me was a nurse who just completed a 12-hour shift at Mayo Clinic. She had fallen asleep at the wheel and plowed into the back of my car. I took a photo of the other car and noticed it was straddling the double yellow line where the road curves to the right. If you continue straight, you cross oncoming traffic and end up in a neighbor's front yard. I prayed about this "accident" and God dropped a thought into my mind. If the other driver had kept going straight, she might have hit another car head-on. I received this impression from God "I put you and your car in the way so I could save her life". It transformed my perspective. It was not a coincidence that I was there, but there was a purpose in it.

The trauma of that accident remained in my subconscious for a long time. I constantly checked my rear-view mirror regardless of whether an approaching car was close. I would get jittery if a car started gaining on me.

Not long after, I participated in a prophetic activity at a "How to Hear God" class. We split into triads where one person would ask God for a picture and describe it to the second person in the group. The second person would interpret the picture for person #3, who was in the "hot seat". I was in the hot seat this time. The first person saw a picture in her mind. It related to me coming out of a dark cave. The interpretation from the second person was "God says, "I've got your back". That interpretation was particularly encouraging in light of the recent accident I had.

In high school, I remember waiting for the school bus with a few other students on a misty morning. We were standing in the middle of a quiet neighborhood street to get a better view. It was foggy and barely drizzling. I felt a tinge of static on my head. Then a BOOM! A thunderous streak of lightning split the air and hit a tall tree some 30 feet away. We were all shaken. We ran to a nearby porch for cover and huddled together. Whew! That was a close call. I was very grateful that we had not been "toasted" that morning!

These events showed that God cares for me.

Even a small event may contain meaning

How many times have you crossed paths with someone at just the right time and just the right place? In 1997, I attended "Stand in the Gap" - a prayer gathering for our country and leaders that drew over a million men to the National Mall in Washington D.C. As we waited for the program to start, I asked God, "If there is someone here that I'm supposed to meet, show me. Don't let me miss them." A few moments later, in the midst of thousands of guys, I looked to the right and noticed an old friend, Gary Warrick, only 20 feet away! Gary led our small group twenty years earlier when both of us lived in Lombard, Illinois. Since that time, I had moved to Rochester, Minnesota, and Gary to Spokane, Washington. I hadn't seen him in years. Not only was that an answer to prayer, but it was the perfect timing and place. That answer to my prayer was not a coincidence!

Looking for God in unexpected places

God is less serious and more fun than we imagine. Traveling minister, Hamilton Filmalter often quips before he illustrates a point, "All seriousness aside...." then he proceeds to illustrate the point with humor. What if God likes to have fun with us during the day? Does that shake your paradigm of who God is? If we are looking for Him, we will find Him "in all the right places".

"Eye has not seen, nor ear heard, nor have entered into the heart of man the things which God has prepared for those who love Him." 1 Cor 2:9. (NKJV)

We often stop quoting this Scripture at this point, expecting that we will never know the wonderful things God has in store for us. However, let's read on...

"But we know about these things because God has sent his Spirit to tell us, and his Spirit searches out and shows us all of God's deepest secrets." 1Cor 2:10 TLB

God wants to show us all sorts of wonders. *"It is God's privilege to conceal things and the king's privilege to discover them."* Prov 25:2 NLT. You have the privilege of discovering God's hidden messages because you are a king or queen. *"But you are a chosen generation, a royal priesthood, a holy nation, His own special people, that you may proclaim the praises of Him who called you out of darkness into His marvelous light.* 1 Peter 2:9 NKJV

Conclusion

WYSIWYG   What You See Is What You Get. What if you could go deeper – to get more than what you see on the surface? What happens when you expect to see more? Your mind will automatically notice that thing subconsciously and alert you to it. This reaction is called the Reticular Activating System (RAS) in the brain. For example, if you just bought a "one of a kind" new outfit to wear to work or school, suddenly you'll notice others who may be wearing a similar outfit.

If you expect to see God's hidden messages, you'll start noticing them everywhere. When you are intentional, instead of drifting through life, your attention will be drawn to the messages.

Recognizing that you live in two worlds - the natural and the spiritual - simultaneously, gives you a new perspective on life. If you aren't aware of the spirit world, you're missing a huge part of life.

One of the first places to look for God's messages is in nature. (See Rom 1:20). God reveals Himself through what He has made. Let's look at some of His creation in the next chapter.

2 Nature: What Can a Storm Tell You?

The wonders of nature reveal a God of awesome beauty and variety. Myriads of stars and thousands of galaxies continue to expand the universe. Scientists keep discovering a smaller and smaller particle that is the essence of all matter. The tiniest insect hunts for food, works, and reproduces. If you develop eyes to see, you will find God's messages here.

Perhaps you've heard of the butterfly effect. It's a theory that proposes that small causes can produce large consequences: A butterfly flapping its wings in Brazil starts a chain of events that could eventually lead to a hurricane in another country. The butterfly effect is derived from chaos theory. Chaos theory tells you there is a purpose in everything that occurs. If you turn your belief from "that was a coincidence" to "there is something behind this event", you'll get a glimpse into the spiritual realm.

The concept of the butterfly effect is a creative metaphor. Metaphoric and symbolic thinking is a gateway beyond the obvious, helping you discover what may be messages from God. He hides messages from your logical thinking. They come into view when you use the creative part of your brain. Using your imagination is key in starting to see differently.

My profession is to always find God in nature. – Henry David Thoreau

Since the creation of the world, His invisible attributes are clearly seen, being understood by the things that are made... (Rom 1:20 NKJV.)

Nature is full of beauty and variety that reveals the character of its Creator -- from the smallest single-celled paramecium to the largest red giant star, such as Betelgeuse. A paramecium is a microscopic organism that can move around, digest food, and reproduce. On the opposite end, Betelgeuse is a huge star in the Orion constellation which, if placed at the center of our solar system, would extend beyond the orbits of Earth, Mars, and possibly Jupiter. What an immense contrast that helps you appreciate the wonder of creation!!

Do you own a favorite photo or painting of a sunset? What draws your attention and inspires you when you're outside in nature?

Is it the brilliant yellows and majestic oranges that burst forth on the trees in autumn? Or the morning song of the lark that awakens you in spring?

Are you awed by the power of Niagara Falls or stunned silent viewing a total eclipse of the sun?

When a summer storm arrives suddenly, does the thunder that vibrates on your chest cause you to shudder in awe?

All these "nature" events reveal the existence of a Creator.

Nature: What Can a Storm Tell You?

In this chapter we'll examine some of the grander, inanimate aspects of the things He created.

Where are you looking?

The other day I caught myself looking down at the asphalt pavement as I walked my dog Emily down the street. Was I watching the pavement pass below me just because it was a gloomy day, or was I simply ignorant of the surrounding beauty trying to express itself to me? Are you too watching the ground more than noticing the world around you? Imagine what you might notice if you turned your gaze to the sky. Are you missing the artistry of heaven? Do you go through life unaware of the world around you? Have you grown complacent because the repetition has caused your senses to go numb?

Join the adventure, change your focus, and start a daily habit of hunting for the treasures in the world around you!

Look! Up in the sky!

The heavens are telling the glory of God; they are a marvelous display of his craftsmanship. Psalm 19:1 TLB

One aspect of nature I enjoy is the sky. As a child, I recall lying on the grass in the front yard on a summer day. I was imagining that the fast-moving cirrocumulus clouds were still and it was us -- the earth -- that was turning instead of the clouds moving. I almost got dizzy as my brain started "feeling" the rotation of the earth.

I'm drawn to the variety of cloud formations. Each day brings a unique view. Do you let the wild clouds capture your attention? As a kid, did you dream up a picture from the constantly changing shapes of clouds? Maybe the cloud you selected resembled a cartoon character, such as Mickey Mouse. Or perhaps you saw an alligator in that elongated stratocumulus cloud.

Have you tried to stop for a moment and observe the clouds? When is the last time you paused, looked heavenward, and let its beauty seep into your spirit? The next time you're outside, take a look at the deep blue sky and thin wispy cirrus clouds high above which might resemble a horse's tail or a pair of snow skis. Let your imagination wander like a child's.

Consider the variety of cloud shapes, sizes, and speeds. The formations you notice today are unique and will never be repeated. Expect another one-of-a-kind panorama of clouds tomorrow. Imagine that God is painting these pictures in the sky just for *you* to discover. What if He's playing a guessing game? "Guess what I'm painting?" "So, you see a cloud in the form of a cat in the sky?" "Yes, I see a cat there." "Do you see his front paws and his round hump in the back, like he is about to pounce on someone?" A few minutes later, the cloud changes shape, and it's no longer a cat. "Now what do you see?" "Take a guess." It's amusing to watch a fast-moving cloud change shape. If you don't have a cell phone or camera to quickly capture the "cat" in the sky, it may turn unto a frog or something entirely different.

Signs in the sky

A few years ago, my pastor attended a leader's conference in California. One speaker declared God was giving us the key. During a break, the leaders pointed to a cloud that had shaped into a key. That's when they also noticed it on their badges. My pastor remarked, "As we were talking about it at our next session, someone pulled an 8-inch key (same style) out of a decorator pot that was sitting in the room." This story is an example of God emphasizing a message He wanted them to hear. It is important to "bend" your ears toward the word and take special note.

The other morning, I rose before sunrise and rushed to the east window in our two-story house. Because we live on the top of a hill, the sky is expansive. Trees frame the sunrises and sunsets and pose for colorful photos.

The horizon began to brighten, broadcasting a variety of colors: aqua, green, and yellow. Was it going to be another gorgeous sunrise? I grabbed my camera and asked Google Home, "What time is sunrise?" I still had a half-hour to enjoy the sky before the sun would break through. The clouds began reflecting a dark red and orange color as the stars and moon faded from view. The sky changed to light pink, followed by a brilliant yellow. Clouds obscured the sun as it rose, but they could not keep light from illuminating the land.

I breathe in the scene and store it in my soul. It refreshes me. Can you picture a similar scene in your mind?

If you are self-conscious occasionally like I am, you might avoid pausing when you're attracted to something in nature. You may miss the beauty around you that refreshes. Does fear of what others might think ever hinder your willingness to pause and absorb the world around you? Raise your eyes to the sky today. Do you see clouds there? If so, take the time to absorb the majesty, the distance, the vastness above. Let the scene inspire you. Practice this exercise to revitalize your spirit. Use your Spirit Eyes.

Count the Stars

Star of wonder star of night, Star with royal beauty bright (from "We Three Kings").

On a clear evening, the wide expanse of the stars and planets calls for my attention. Bob, one of my neighbors, has a

Nature: What Can a Storm Tell You?

home-made observatory I've visited. Gazing at the sky through Bob's telescope has given me an even greater appreciation for the magnificence of the night sky (and I've also developed a friendship with Bob, a bonus!)

The night sky becomes clearer the farther you live from a big city, where the lights and haze obscure your view. In the winter, the stars display even more vibrancy and clarity. On a moonless night, the longer you look, the more stars you can see. When star-gazing, look to one side or the other of a star cluster and you'll detect more stars, such as the Pleiades, which is a cluster of seven stars that are visible all over the world.

Have you ever tried to count the stars? Kids will give it a try. God asked Abraham to count them. He took Abraham outside and said, "Look up at the sky and count the stars--if indeed you can count them." (NIV). There are too many to comprehend!

Space is big. *Really, really, really big.* With the naked eye, we can see only a fraction of the millions of stars in the Milky Way, our galaxy. The distance between any two stars is so immense that collisions are out of the question. The nearest star to us, Alpha Centauri, is 4.3 light-years away (25 trillion miles). To appreciate the distance between the earth and Alpha Centauri, consider how long it would take to travel to this star. What is your guess? The New Horizons spacecraft, traveling at 36,000 mph, would take over 70,000 years to reach this star! That's unfathomable. There seems to be no end to the vastness of the universe which is still expanding. Astronomers have estimated the number of stars in our Milky Way galaxy at 100 to 250 billion. Our galaxy is only one of over 100 to 200 billion galaxies. These numbers are astounding.

A great big, good God created these celestial bodies. We can enjoy them, sense the Creator's grandeur, and reflect on the nearness of our God.

Mountains

I grew up in the Midwest where plains are abundant, with little change in the terrain -- and certainly no mountains. It was boring in a way, just plain. Maybe that's why we call these level places *plains*.

The mountains first grabbed my attention when my wife, Betty, and I went on our honeymoon trip to the Canadian Rockies. Excitement gripped me when mountains came into view. Betty and I both took many pictures with our 35mm film cameras, at a time when film was expensive. It was worth it. We counted at least 22 pictures of the Crowfoot Glacier – we must have been impressed!

Driving through the mountains and absorbing their beauty was a new experience for us mid-westerners, thus the reason for "capturing the memories" on film. Mountains are big, or as you might say, "ginormous". You can spot them in the distance as you drive toward them. You feel like you'll be at their feet in minutes. Two hours later, you're still driving toward the same mountain range.

The closer you get to the mountains, the more majestic they appear, the more towering they become, and they may even look foreboding. No wonder man has sought to conquer them! When I slow down to contemplate how high and wide these massive rocks are, I am awed by the greatness of God.

Are there mountains in sight near your home?

If you live in the plains, far from mountains, there's another way to imagine them. Near sunset, the clouds appear as if they were a string of mountains on the horizon. Can you imagine the layer of clouds in the distance being a mountain range? They are certainly large enough.

If you live in the plains, you might enjoy the mountains, the ocean, and other parts of nature that you don't see near your home. For example, if your home is in West Texas, you might enjoy exploring a forest or going mountain climbing. I remember driving for hours in Central Texas without seeing a single tree. Finally, I spotted a tree. It stood alone – the only one surviving for miles on this wide flatland. We grow accustomed to nature that is close to our home not because it's not worthy of our attention, but because it's become commonplace. Here is an example.

The places near you that you take for granted are site-seeing opportunities for guests. Visitors sometimes ask me about places near our city of Rochester that I have never seen myself, such as The Plummer House, a vintage building, Spark (a children's museum), or a local restaurant such as Newt's. I'm almost embarrassed to admit "I've never been there, but I've heard it's great". You may be living near one of God's natural wonders: the ocean, the mountains, forests, deserts, lakes, waterfalls, rock formations, or plains full of wheat and corn. Which of these nature sites have you taken for granted?

A summer thunderstorm

Thunder startles me, especially at night when I'm jolted awake by a nearby lightning strike. Sometimes it feels like the next lightning bolt will hit our house. Our house is high up on a hill, so this is a definite possibility – and lightning has struck two nearby houses in the past.

When a summer storm is brewing, I like to step out on the front deck where I'm protected from the rain. From this vantage point, far away clouds light up as bolts of light dance from cloud to cloud between them. The wind picks up and I hear pellets of rain hitting the ground with a sound like pea gravel makes when a kid throws it on a slide. The trees bend in the blowing wind and chills climb up my arms as the temperature suddenly drops. The wind refreshes me as it wipes across my sweaty face and cools me down. When the lightning gets closer and claps of thunder vibrate across my chest, I return to the shelter indoors.

Lightning is powerful. It's violent enough to fry electric appliances if it hits near your home. This happened to two of our neighbors a few years ago when lightning struck the ground between their houses across the street from us. It's fortunate that homes near us sprawl out in two- to -three-acre lots.

Sometimes you can smell burning rubber from a transformer that just blew or see the havoc created when large limbs of trees crashed to the ground following lightning strikes. The strength of storms reminds me of the power of God.

What message is God sending us through the storms? He protects us from the physical damage of the summer storm and also leads us through the storms in our lives.

Let it Snow or That's enough!

Spring? The calendar may show it's April, but here in Minnesota, it can still snow several inches. Snow is ferocious when it whips sideways during a blizzard. I experience this every year in an up-close and personal way: The wind is seldom calm when I'm wrestling the snow blower down our 100-foot driveway to clear the snow. When I reach the street and turn the snow blower around to trudge back to house, whoosh! – a gust of wind spits a spray of snow right in my face. My cheeks feel ice-cold, and drops of melting snow cascade down my scarf as I frantically swivel the snow discharge chute in the opposite direction. It's a chilling experience, but one I'm now accustomed to.

On the other hand, snow can be beautiful when it's softly falling in flakes that have bundled together in larger clumps. I stick out my tongue to catch some of those fluffy flakes. I open my glove to catch them. If I'm gentle, I can capture snowflakes without breaking them. When I examine them closely, I marvel at the beauty of each unique flake - a six-sided crystal. Amazing! No two snowflakes are alike.

I admire the variety in this feature of nature. It unveils something about the character of God. He is not in a hurry when he creates. He creates originals all the time. No two snowflakes are alike. No two leaves are alike. No two clouds are alike. No two sunsets are alike. No two tomato seeds are alike. You could list many items that we tend to think of as "the same" when in reality no two are identical. You aren't like anyone else either. You are a unique creation of God!

Observing nature is a great way for you to connect with God, your Creator and uncover His messages to you. With a little intentionality on your part, the wonders of nature can rejuvenate your soul.

Exercises

- Ask God to show you the meaning of what you are experiencing in the natural. Once you begin to intentionally observe, you will start recognizing God's messages for you. If you are at a loss of what to say, try this: *"God, show me the beauty of the world beyond the surface. Whisper your messages to me in a way I can understand. I come to you with an open mind ready to see the world with new eyes. Please give me 'Spirit Eyes.'"*
- Identify what you gravitate toward in nature - plants, animals, sky, lakes, trees, mountains, hills, scenery, etc. Look for these scenes or events when you're outside. Visit a zoo and take your time enjoying your favorite exhibits. Don't worry about seeing everything. Go outside regardless of the season and discover something you can appreciate.
- How can you better appreciate the vastness of the universe? Find an astronomy club or community education group in your area that offers a class. Take advantage of visiting a planetarium in a high school or college near you.

3 Art: Can a Painting Leave You Breathless?

Artists may portray a picture of God, angels, and heaven, but has a piece of art struck you with awe yet had no obvious spiritual content? Why do tears fill your eyes when gazing at one painting but another one holds no appeal?

Nature provides limitless subjects for artists: mountains, lakes, trees, soaring eagles, busy beavers, rushing streams, and more.

What messages can we uncover in art?

What is art?

The Oxford Dictionary defines art as the expression or application of human creative skill and imagination, typically in a visual form such as painting or sculpture, producing works to be appreciated primarily for their beauty or emotional power.

As a math and science person, I admit that I've had to expand my narrow definition of art beyond painting. Paintings were all I noticed while visiting the Art Institute of Chicago during a school field trip. More recently, I began appreciating paintings more when I observed art that moved my heart. Akiane was one of those artists, whom I first found online.

Akiane Kramarik, now a world-famous artist, began painting with no formal training. Her painting "Prince of Peace" which she painted at age 8 brings Jesus to life. It is a composite of some of the heavenly visions she experienced. I call this type of spirit-inspired art "Prophetic Art" because it is created during a time of worship or connection with the Creator. This spiritual art infuses your soul with emotion. It pulls you into an experience versus just observing a painting. You can find an entire gallery of Akiane's art at https://akiane.com/. The famous "Prince of Peace" painting can be viewed here https://akiane.com/product/prince-of-peace/.

A pastor friend of mine, Connie, told me a story that illustrates the power of God-inspired art. When Connie attended a pastors' conference, she heard about a woman who had been diagnosed with stage IV cancer. A "prophetic" painting at church caught her attention. She lingered in front of it for several minutes absorbed in its beauty. The painting called "Hope" affected her deeply. Like a spark, it awakened something in her that had been dormant. Hope ignited. At her next doctor's visit, the test results revealed that her tumors were shrinking. Eventually, they totally disappeared. She was completely healed!

Every year I attend a prophetic conference in Minneapolis and have the privilege of watching a professional artist in action. Janet Hyun paints during the worship sessions, which last about an hour each morning and evening. She employs a unique painting method: She starts applying color blotches with a 2-inch brush onto a black canvas and refines the painting step-by-step using finer-point brushes.

Art: Can a Painting Leave You Breathless?

Janet's art inspires me. "The Glory Horse" that she painted during a worship session was particularly powerful. The same painting awed my wife, and we now own a print of it. It's. It similar to a painting called "Glory Chasers" that you can see in Janet's online gallery at http://www.JanetHyun.com.

Take time to linger in front of a masterpiece and let its beauty seep into your soul. An artist projects not only his/her emotions but also beliefs onto a canvas. Not every masterpiece will speak to you in the same way.

I am not an art connoisseur, but I do have an aversion to abstract art that projects chaos, such as an abstract Picasso painting. Over the years his self-portraits evolved to become very abstract, from a realistic painting of a young man at 15, to a grotesque-looking abstract figure at age 90. I feel a knot in my stomach and tightness in my head when I view this Cubist artwork. Akiane's work, In contrast gives me a feeling of lightness and rest. Picasso's straight lines, sudden angles, squares, and triangles clash when joined to resemble a mechanical face, not something that resembles the curves common to one's face -- that describes his second self-portrait painted at age 90. You may find these images online by searching "Pablo Picasso self-portraits over time". https://bobyewchuk.wordpress.com/2017/06/08/picasso/

To me, Picasso's paintings are in stark contrast to the prophetic art from Akiane Kramaric, Janet Hyun or Lyn Lasneski. Just as writers have a message to convey, artists send a message through their medium of oil, acrylic or water colors. On her website http://www.Janethyun.com, Janet says, "I want to change our cultural atmosphere so it contains good, positive energy from the Spirit." You can recognize Janet's beliefs reflected in her paintings.

Victory - Janet Hyun

Do you limit definition of art to drawings and paintings as I've done? We mentioned how God paints pictures in the sky with the clouds. Nature produces an abundance of art for us to enjoy. Besides paintings, some other forms of man-made art include sculpting and architecture.

Sculpting is a complex process that takes time and can be very expensive depending on the materials used. A friend of mine, Kat Hitzeman, is a sculpture artist who creates beautiful dancing figures, which can take weeks and even months to complete. Kat is a member of the Society of Minnesota Sculptors. You can find more about Kat at her website: http://kaleidoscopeeyestosee.weebly.com/

Art: Can a Painting Leave You Breathless?

Here are a couple of her masterpieces.

Miriam - Kate Hitzeman

Beauty for Ashes - Kate Hitzeman

Rookery Building, Chicago ,©Felix Lipov

What about architecture? Can buildings be considered art as well? An architect produces a blueprint before a building is erected. He or she sketches the building and fills in the dimensions of every wall, staircase, window, and door. You can appreciate the artistry of famous architects such as Frank Lloyd Wright or in city skyscrapers which have not only practical and mechanical stability but also possess an aesthetic appeal. Although they are man-made structures, you can view these artistic structures beyond just looking at the surface.

I am training myself to observe more intentionally the everyday, common objects I view. One technique I use is asking questions: What else is there in this sculpture that I do not notice at first sight? Does this sculpture have symbolic meaning? Is there meaning beyond the obvious? Depending on where you've grown up, you may have been surrounded by fields, forests, or in a neighborhood with houses set close together. As I mentioned earlier, your view of something less familiar will pique your curiosity more than the familiar. If you grew up on the plains, mountains will attract you. If you are used to seeing mountains from living near them, they won't seem like a big deal. In the same way, if you grew up in the city, tall buildings may have been common. You can look at common structures such as skyscrapers with Spirit Eyes when you become curious and ask "I wonder" questions. When you slow down and become intentional in observing, you will uncover deeper meaning. It takes time to truly observe, so don't be in a hurry. Take a second look. Ask questions, search for meaning.

 Here's an example from my life: I grew up in the suburbs of Chicago, and although downtown Chicago was only 15 miles away, we seldom visited that area. When I recall buildings that awed me at that time, I think of the Prudential building, a 40-story office building that was acclaimed as the tallest in Chicago in the 1960s. A few years later, the 100-story John Hancock Center (now called 875 North Michigan Avenue) and the Sears Tower (now called Willis Tower) achieved recognition as the tallest buildings in Chicago. The Willis Tower remained the tallest building in the world until 2013. These skyscrapers are not only functional, but each has its own unique beauty.

 Riding an elevator to the observation deck in one of these tall buildings, you are greeted with a birds-eye view of the city. In Chicago, you enjoy a view of Lake Michigan. You'll spot the boats sailing on the lake. You might identify a larger vessel on the horizon. Panning the area, you'll notice airplanes below – especially single-engine planes, a few landing or taking off from Mitchell Field (Milwaukee Mitchell International Airport), an airport on the lake. Surveying the area at this height is the next best thing to flying!

 When a new building is proposed, architects compete to win a contract for the best design. What characteristics of skyscrapers speak to you? I'm enamored by their immense height. I admire their brilliant silver color and the numerous windows. I notice how the buildings sway in the wind especially at the higher levels. That flexibility enables them to withstand strong winds.

Here is where I dig deeper and use my imagination: How might these characteristics symbolically relate to me? Just as a skyscraper is tall and needs to bend in order not to break, I am tall and I need to be flexible too. It reminds me of a quote that was posted in the front of the bus on one of my mission trips to Mexico with Darrell Dobbelmann of Dove International: "He who remains flexible will not be bent out of shape." It's good advice!

Art: Can a Painting Leave You Breathless?

Exercises

- Whether you're an art connoisseur or not, developing curiosity is a prerequisite to discovering how art can touch your soul. You don't need to visit an art museum to experience the energy behind art. You can recognize the art in a restaurant, at a store, in an office, at work, or in a nursing home to develop your spiritual discernment.
- How do you define art? Is it sketches, paintings, sculptures, or more? Write down your current definition and start adding to that list.
- Check out these artists online: Akiane Kramarik, Janet Hyun, Lyn Lasneski.

SPIRIT EYES

4 Signs: Finding Direction When You're Lost

Storefront signs, highway signs, and billboards are placed to grab your attention. Discover significance in these examples: Welcome, North Carolina; WhyNaught Road; Liberty, Missouri. What deeper sense can you derive from these names?

A world without signs

I magine a world without signs. You're driving on a highway and a car is coming straight toward you. It sounds like a bad dream. What country are you in? There is no sign to indicate if this is a one-way street or not. You have no idea if you should drive on the right or left side of the road. It would be utter chaos without signs - no *Speed Limit* signs, no direction signs, warning signs, no street signs, and so on. It would be a fruitless search to find a specific house. Where would you exit the freeway? How would you enter the freeway, especially if you saw cars coming up the ramp you were going down? We need signs.

I was driving to a conference in Arkansas a couple of years ago when I passed a highway sign for the city of Liberty, Missouri. It immediately caught my attention because my granddaughter is named Liberty. In my mind, I pictured myself showing Liberty a photo of the sign and telling her that she had a city named after her!

What's behind the name *Liberty*? What possibilities did I consider? Some obvious examples are Freedom, the Liberty Bell, *"With liberty and justice for all"*, and the Statue of Liberty. What ideas do you have?

Liberty or freedom is a gift from God. Our country is founded on freedom: Freedom to express yourself without fear of retaliation or imprisonment; freedom to believe whatever you want in regards to your faith; freedom to support a party's political platform; freedom to choose a career; freedom to live wherever you choose; freedom to assemble. You have the freedom to travel to any city anytime, whether domestic travel or overseas. Freedom the travel is something to be thankful for. People in other countries such as China do not have the freedom to travel. Consider all that the word "Liberty" might convey to you if you spotted this sign on your journey. What other words have deep meaning to you?

Just off I-90 in southwest Minnesota, you will come across a city called "Welcome, Minnesota". My friend John lives there. It's a small town, but I'd be intrigued to visit it and learn the history behind the city. What kind of people would you expect to meet in Welcome? What other intriguing names of cities come to your mind?

Some signs are humorous. I once saw a sign in New York state that read "Road Construction next 154 miles". I think the decimal point was covered up because 100+ miles of construction is ludicrous! Another sign popped up on my GPS recently.

It was "Whynaught Court". Clever! There are only a couple of commercial buildings on Whynaught Court, no residential ones. Why was it named "Whynaught"? Let's imagine. Perhaps one of the first builders questioned whether this was a good location and was attracted by the affordable price of the land. Maybe he quipped "Why not? Why not build here. This could be a great location." Or perhaps it is a play on the word "naught". Will it all be for naught? Will building here be the wrong thing for us?

Does "why not" speak to you? Have you been stalled on a project that's been on your mind for a long time? Have you been procrastinating on fulfilling a desire such as a trip you hope to take or a renovation you have not completed? Have you yet to invite a friend over for dinner? Why not?

I'm describing written signs, but we're all aware of other highway symbols such as traffic lights, caution lights, yield signs, and stop signs. Before you pass your driver's license test you learn to recognize the meaning of a sign from its geometric shape. Even if the words were obliterated, you would recognize a stop sign or yield sign. The shape is a symbol of the meaning of the sign. The meaning is conveyed without words.

Signs as answers to prayer

A friend of mine, Carol, shared this story after a mission trip to Guatemala. It is here with her permission:

Our team walked into a shop that displayed a shrine of Maximon, a Mayan deity. We sensed an evil presence there. Cecil, the leader of our missions' group, felt led to have us all make declarations, plus to laugh over the shrine, using the verse from Psalm 2:4: "He Who sits in the heavens laughs. The Lord makes fun of them." After making our declarations and laughing, we knew we needed to sing something but didn't know what. Someone started singing "I Exalt Thee". We all joined in. The atmosphere turned peaceful as we finished the song.

Later, when we asked each other "Who started that song? Did you?," each person replied, "No, I didn't. Wasn't it you?" We concluded that angels were present and had started the song. After returning home driving near Stewartville, Minnesota, I had doubts in my mind --did I make up this stuff? I looked up in time to spot a billboard that read "You Can't Make This Stuff Up!" That was a dramatic answer to my doubt.

An event can be a sign

In ancient writings, a sign might be an event that was visible to many people at the same time. In our culture, this "vision" or apparition might be considered a coincidence or hallucination because we are less accepting of spiritual events. The scientific method we've adopted requires an event to be observable and repeatable. In ancient times, people would accept a vision or apparition as a spiritual event. It was not only considered supernatural, but real. Signs were prophesied in the writings of the prophet Isaiah. *Unto you, a child will be born. He will be ruler over all the nations. This shall be a sign to you: A virgin will conceive and bring forth a son.* This child was the Messiah or Savior of Israel. The Israelites were looking for a literal king to deliver them from the slavery of the Roman Empire. They did not possess the Spirit Eyes to see from a symbolic or spiritual vantage point. The true savior or "anointed one" was not a political king but a spiritual king. Jesus replied to Pilate's question with, "Yes, I am a king, but My kingdom is not of the earth realm." Wouldn't that freak you out if you were Pilate? The people missed Jesus because they failed to see the full purpose of his coming.

Purpose of Signs – What's the big deal?

What is the purpose of a sign? *A sign is not the end in itself. It points to something greater, more real. It gives you direction.* This is particularly true when you observe signs in the sky – a rainbow for instance. God set his rainbow in the sky as a promise that he would never again destroy the earth with a flood. (He even reminds Himself!)

Are there other places God posts messages for us? A sign for a store called "Golden Boys" once caught my attention. "I'm not sure what that place does, but I found myself attracted to the symbolism. Why "Golden"? I look for positive meanings. Gold is valuable. What could that mean to me personally? I have four boys (sons). Is God reminding me to view them as valuable because that is how He sees them? What does "Golden Boys" mean to you?

I'm not suggesting trying to fabricate meaning out of everything you see. It works best when you can relax and are expectant. You are more likely to find messages in a leisurely moment when you are not hurried.

I've mentioned how signs direct us or warn you. What happens when you miss observing one of those signs? If it's a highway sign, you may end up in an accident or you may get a ticket from a policeman for failing to observe the speed limit or for parking illegally. If we misinterpret a speed limit sign in a country that uses the metric system, that could be a problem as well. It's important to learn the language of the culture when interpreting a sign.

Ships have flags to identify who they are and to communicate with other vessels. The order and number of flags used determine the message. You must have the key to decipher those flag symbols. Your Friend above loves to play hide-and-seek. It's your job to find and decipher the love messages He's left specifically for you. (See Proverbs 25:2)

What if God is speaking to you through a sign and you fail to see it? What are the repercussions? Many of the messages I recognize from God indicate "I'm glad to be with you." "I love communicating with you in a personal way." "Do you see My messages?" The way you interpret these personal messages depends on how you view God. Is He a God who enjoys sharing life with you or is He intent on making sure you obey the rules?

I remember a day coaching kids' soccer practice. The light rain stopped, the sun came out, and a rainbow appeared in the eastern sky. One of the players exclaimed, "Look, a rainbow!". It's a joyful experience to stop and take in the sight. I could have ignored the player's exclamation of delight and continued with the practice, but I took a breather to stop. "Let's stop and enjoy the rainbow a moment." We started describing what each of us saw for a minute and it became a happy memory for all of us as a group.

Some signs are a warning, some are to give us direction and some are for information and enjoyment. Wall Drug is a tourist attraction located in the town of Wall, South Dakota. It is a shopping mall consisting of a drug store, gift shop, restaurants, and various other stores. Wall Drug earns much of its fame from its self-promotion. Many visitors of Wall Drug have erected signs throughout the world announcing the distance to Wall Drug in miles. You will see billboards all across the state enticing you to stop, hundreds of them. If there were only one, who would stop? But the sheer number of them makes you curious.

Inspirational signs
The following quotes don't need interpretation. Pick one that speaks to you:
Mistakes prove that you are trying.
Today is a good day to have a good day.
Blessed.
It always seems impossible until it's done.
Don't look back…You're not going that way.
Kindness matters.
You are stronger than you think. Never give up.
Whether you think you can or can't. You're right.

Exercises

- Be aware when a sign catches your eye. Start by being intentional. God always rewards His friends who look for Him. Ask questions about what you see. Does that sign have a deeper meaning? Is that God giving me a wink? What is He saying? Does that sign have symbolic meaning for me?
- Begin to observe the objects around you more symbolically. What can they represent? What is the hidden message behind the sign you're observing that might be God speaking to you?

5 Music: How Does the Melody Move You?

Lyrics in music are often self-explanatory, but the melody affects our emotions. What causes one song to produce tears but another entices you to stand up and dance? Certain music triggers a connection from your soul to a God who loves you. How do you respond when you feel the spirit behind the music?

How does music speak to you?

A few years ago, my wife and I were headed to "Family Camp" with two of our grandchildren. The song "Write Your Story" by Francesca Battistelli was playing in the car. and I intended to play the entire CD. When the song ended, the grandkids begged, "Play it again, please." The theme of "Write Your Story" is summed up in these lines: "I'm an empty page, an open book, Won't You write Your story on my heart?" It's an invitation for God to make you new, place

His mark on your life. I felt a bit edgy as my brow wrinkled and my mouth turned tense with a frown. I only got away with playing one additional song on the CD before I was out-voted and relented to their request. We played the song over and over – six times or more.

Why do kids want to hear the same song over and over again? I thought it was childish, but after a long time, I reconsidered. If a song increases your joy, gives you happy feelings, you don't want it to end, do you? I'm learning to be child-like and have more fun. We want those enjoyable moments to last. I can now give myself permission to act like a kid and "Play it again and again." If it brings me joy, I will replay the song a few times. Why not treat yourself to that option the next time you're listening to a song on your playlist that gives you energy, encouragement, or inspiration? God gave you music to enrich your life. When you enjoy that gift, it's like telling Him "Thank you!"

Music awakens emotions

Music affects your brain. It has been shown to elevate intelligence, relax the body, including reducing blood pressure and pain. It impacts memory and increases mental alertness. Happy music affects the way we see someone's face. Some types of music increase our creativity.

It's close to Christmas as I write this chapter, the time of year when we start hearing Christmas music playing in stores. I found my favorite custom-made playlist (a CD) with songs I loved to listen to a decade ago. The first song transported me back to a cold winter day walking to the train station. It was a different season of life, as our kids were young and I was early in my career with IBM. The feelings came back as I relived that scene in my imagination. The lyrics were as meaningful as when I first heard the song.

When you listen to an old song, have you ever found yourself in a memory of the place where you first heard that song? Some songs invite you into the nearness of God. This music resonates with your spirit and the words magnify your experience. One of my favorite places to enjoy music is in the car, which has excellent acoustics. I loosen up and interact with singers such as TobyMac, Lauren Daigle, or Crowder. I engage with their songs which entice you to sing, move, and dance. On the other hand, if I'm listening to slower music, I feel relaxed and peaceful. Music is a powerful tool to engage our emotions. How does God speak to you through music?

Can music give you direction?

I heard a Kim Walker-Smith song on the radio the other day but thought it was my car CD playing because it was a new song I recently purchased. I noticed the same song -- "Fresh Outpouring" -- playing again while driving to a breakfast meeting the next day. After lunch, the song was playing in my head as I turned on the radio. The same song was playing again! Was that a coincidence? That evening, at a team meeting to discuss our church's plans for the upcoming year, I shared my experience of hearing that song so many times that day. The song content aligned with the direction we were discussing. The song speaks of longing for a fresh experience from God. We were feeling that a shift was coming. People are weary of dissension, division, and hateful social media posts. They are hungry for unity and togetherness. Yes, we need a fresh outpouring of peace and harmony. This song reinforced the message to continually seek God and be open to change.

Can genres make a difference?

Music comes in a variety of genres: jazz, folk, rock, hip hop, blues, classical, country, easy-listening, and more. Each genre conveys its unique culture.

Country music is sometimes associated with sad lyrics, where the singer has lost a lot in life. A favorite joke is "What do you get when you play country music backward?" Answer: "You get back your wife, your dog, and your pickup."

Classical music has been known to inspire creativity. Artists and writers use this type of instrumental music while they are writing or painting.

Rock music can stir up feelings of excitement, freedom, edginess. Screaming vocals and distorted guitar chords may grate on your nerves.

Contemporary Christian music that is mellow in style may bring you a sense of peace. It can also lift your spirit or bring tears to your eyes. The emotions you experience are examples of non-verbal communication between you and God.

Similar to the improvisation of jazz and blues, spontaneous songs are now popular in worship settings such as IHOPKC, and other 24/7 worship centers as well as vibrant churches.

Pay attention to the genre and the tone the melody brings to your soul. Each genre carries the message its own cultural context. What genre influences you?

Is there a place for quiet?

Music that is majestic and wonderful and can move us deeply, but it's also important to remember that we need quiet and not become addicted to always having something playing in a way that it becomes more like "noise" than praise. You don't have to look far to recognize that we are bombarded with media including videos and music no matter where you go. Gas stations, Walmart, and hobby stores all have music playing. The still small voice of God can be drowned by all this sensory stimulation. A place of quiet can enhance your receptors to hear His messages more clearly.

Several years ago, I attended a conference that addressed the effects of rock music as well as other topics. The speaker illustrated the impact of various types of music on your soul. He especially pointed to the effects of dissonant hard rock or heavy metal music that grates on your emotions. He said the melody carries the message, not just the lyrics alone. It's interesting to consider how often we cannot decipher the lyrics of a song, but we accept the full package because we're captivated by the melody.

I like songs where the lyrics are clear and understandable, where you can sing along if you so desire. I believe that both the melody (meaning the rhythm, score, tune, and chords) as well as the lyrics are important. When these elements mesh well, you receive the full impact of the song. The message as a whole will either be positive or negative - giving life or producing death.

Did I get those lyrics right?

As a junior high student, I memorized the lyrics of songs with what I thought were the right words. Years later when the song was sung, I realized I had heard incorrectly. Some words I thought I heard did not even exist. (At least I got the lyrics to Y-M-C-A correct!) We all have selective hearing in some way. None of us hears perfectly, but that's what makes us unique individuals to whom God can speak in such a specific way that we begin to realize "He knows me!"

Some music has a beat and rhythm that is catchy. One such song is from "The Lego Movie 2: The Second Part" and is titled *"Catchy Song"*. The most catchy line is *"This Song is Gonna Get Stuck Inside Your Head."* The 10-hour version of this song on YouTube had over a million hits in one month.

Melancholy, Mad, or Majestic Melodies?

Songs written in a minor key can bring us into a melancholy emotion, which may be sad or somber. They cause you to reminisce. Songs in a minor key can also evoke a need to change, to move forward into something greater in your life. Minor chords can be enticing and create a feeling of well-being, but songs don't end with a minor chord because it sounds unresolved. God can speak in these minor keys to move you to change, turn yourself around, or feel regret for some previous mistake you made.

Dissonant chords such as major seventh chords are beautiful, but they move us toward another chord to resolve the dissonance, usually a major chord. Major chords sound full and final. You'll find them at the beginning and end of a piece. They create a feeling of majesty, royalty, importance, and give a feeling of pride. That sound can incite you to stand up. These chords are effective when you are viewing God as a King, Creator, or Majestic. Songs usually finish with a major chord, a feeling of completion. Understanding these various chords can help explain why you experience different emotions depending on the music.

Your mood will determine what kind of music you feel like playing. We often choose music that synchronizes with our current feelings. If you recognize your feeling and want to move out of it, you can change your mood by purposely choosing a different type or genre of music. Soft music or loud music? Fast or slow? Instrumental or vocal? These are ways to categorize a song. For example, you can chase away depression and melancholy emotions by selecting lively hip-hop songs.

Exercises

- What is one song you like so much that you would like to play it over and over? Do you like the lyrics more than the melody, or do you prefer the melody? What songs appeal to you? Can you find a theme in them? Pick three songs you enjoy. Write them down. Check out the lyrics, sense the melodies. Look for a common theme between them. What do you find?
- Listen not only to the lyrics but the spirit behind the music itself – see what message the melody carries. Does the melody of the song convey the message well? Hint: Search YouTube for "New Songs Café" or "Behind the song" where the writer explains the story behind the song.
- What music inspires you? Classical symphonies? Themes from musicals? Discover what music inspires you to creativity.

6 Video: Hidden Messages Revealed

From video games to YouTube, the world is not bereft of eye-appealing visual entertainment. Can you find hidden messages in the world of entertainment? Music video clips bring vocalists' songs to life and enable them to share their vision with an on-demand audience.

One of my favorite things to watch on TV is the Olympics and after that, the Paralympics. Athletes train their whole lives to compete for the ultimate award – a medal distinguishing them as the best in the world in their sport. The commercials aired during these broadcasts are either sports-related or motivational, including messages not solely meant to persuade you to purchase a product. Some will pull on your heartstrings to change a belief or inspire you. These are feel-good messages. The final seconds of the ad project the company's slogan. Examples: We help you do what can't be done *#DoWhatYouCant" (Samsung); When you're free to *move, anything is possible; Start your impossible" (Toyota);* and *Win from within (Gatorade).*

Music Videos

Music videos became popular the late 1980s on MTV. Now we can view them on demand on YouTube. These artistic expressions are particularly powerful because they require the use of both parts of your brain. The lyrics are verbal (a left-brain task), and the video is visual (a right-brain task). Music also impacts our emotions, which is another reason we remember a particular song so well.

If I could pick any song as the theme of this book, I would choose TobyMac's "Everything". When you watch the music video on YouTube, you can see the story behind the lyrics. As the video demonstrates, when we put on rose-colored glasses or use our "Spirit Eyes," we see the potential in each person. I call that the treasure in them. We see the good hidden inside instead of only their outward appearance.

Take note of the music videos that tug at your heart. Delve into the underlying meaning. That's the left-side or logical part of your brain. When you combine both left-brain and right-brain thinking, you become a richer person. You grow. Keep growing. Never stop learning. There is always something new to learn, something more to enrich life, something more to enhance your maturity.

What about cartoons and animated films?

Visual images directed toward young viewers are purposely created with a message to influence children's values and beliefs. Political issues are evident in cartoons. Protect-the-environment and Save-the-earth messages are part of many animated features. Some examples are "WALL-E" (garbage will bury us all) and "Happy Feet," a penguin movie implying we are overfishing the Antarctic waters, which hurts penguins by taking away their food source. Other movies showing a positive message are "Frozen" (Only an active of true love with thaw a frozen heart) and "Smallfoot", which encourages you to accept others who are not the same as you. We need to be discerning on which movies are spreading values we hold true and which are influencing our children contrary to our beliefs. I go into more depth of messages in movies in the Movies chapter.

How to discover more messages

Do you get hooked watching videos? The attraction of watching video is probably common among creative folks or right-brained thinkers. It's easier to recall visual impressions than written content. The brain is built this way. You may forget a written explanation, but when you view it as a moving picture (video, TV, movie, etc.), you remember it better. Why? Because a picture is worth... yes, a thousand words.

YouTube is one of the most popular platforms for video content. YouTube used to be free, but now ads are inserted into nearly every video. After you view a clip, you are shown several "suggested for you" options. Your curiosity draws you to watch these video clips because they relate to your interests. These videos can be distractions or pull you in a negative direction. They can be a waste of time – or a time of unexpected discovery. Do these suggestions reflect your values? I often enjoy playing worship music on YouTube. I've discovered songs published years ago that I've never heard before, but they are fresh-sounding and lively. I feel God's pleasure when I listen to these newly-discovered pieces. This is a "win" for me.

Am I encouraging you to waste hours looking for a song or video? Not at all. I've experienced getting side-tracked more than once. On the other hand, I become more open to new ideas as I explore. Every kid likes to explore and discover. That is one of the positive aspects of becoming childlike (not childish). Keep learning and never stop. When you expect to find more messages, you will.

Some years ago in early spring, I was hiking with my son Joel on a little-used trail around a lake. We almost stepped on what looked like a dead black branch when the branch twitched and quickly slithered away. The snake scared us, but it wasn't large. A few minutes later we thought we saw another skinny snake that was not moving. As we crept up closer, we recognized it as a long bent black stick – not a living thing at all!

In the same way, when we anticipate God is hiding messages for us to discover every day, we're more apt to "see" things differently. Dig for the deeper meaning in what catches your eye. Get curious. Ask God questions. "Why am I suspicious of the superhero in that film?" for instance. Slow down occasionally to smell the flowers. You will be rewarded.

Commercials

Networks select commercials based on viewer demographics of each particular program. For example, if you're watching a football game, you'll see beer and truck commercials. The networks select these specific ads expecting that the audience is mainly young males who enjoy these items. You won't see truck and beer commercials on the Hallmark Channel. Instead, there are many medical drug-related commercials and geriatric-themed spots.

Video: Hidden Messages Revealed

Commercials aired during the Paralympics are especially captivating. Be sure to check out the commercials during the next Olympics or Paralympics event. The stories depicting athletes overcoming their handicaps and coming back from injuries will inspire you.

Consider snowboarding Paralympian Mike Schultz. Mike loved to race BMX bikes, then moved into snowmobile racing. When he tragically lost one of his legs in a near-death snowmobile accident, he thought his career in sports was over and was happy just to learn to walk again. But his prosthetic didn't have the range of motion he wanted, and it didn't fit well. That's when he decided to take his problem-solving abilities into the garage and prosthetic design into his own hands. Mike had experience working on racing equipment, and he knew the athletic side and body mechanics, so it was a perfect match for him to begin working on a better prosthetic.

Mike developed a cushioned knee system around a mountain bike shock and learned to snowboard as an amputee. He entered into snowboarding as a product developer, and when snowboarding became a Paralympic sport in 2014, Mike became a competitor.

Mike did not let his tragedy get the best of him. He viewed his handicap not as a career-ending event, but as an opportunity to help others who had suffered a similar loss. In a similar manner, you can begin to view life's challenges as opportunities. That is the message I drew from this story. What is the message for you?

Samsung commercials inspire us as well. A few years ago, Samsung released a commercial showing an ostrich in the desert who, while eating scraps off a table, suddenly finds a virtual reality headset on her head. The VR headset plays the Flight Simulator program while the player of the game flies through the clouds. You can hear Elton John's singing "Rocket Man" as the ostrich sees herself flying in the sky. Ostriches cannot fly, but this bird doesn't know that. She keeps believing and trying well into the night. Her belief creates "Spirit Eyes". In the morning we see the bird without the headset – an artificial intelligence mechanism. She senses a shift in the wind and decides now is the time. As she gains speed, we see her legs lift off the ground, and we see her shadow on the ground as she begins to fly. The other ostriches gawk in wonder. Samsung concludes the commercial with *"We make what can't be made, so you can do what can't be done."* The ad ends with the hashtag #DoWhatYouCan't.

It's significant that the bird no longer has the VR headset on. She puts away the fantasy of virtually flying and transitions to actually doing it because she used Spirit Eyes. This is one of my favorite commercials. It inspires me and gives me a hope deep inside -- and a challenge. We were made for something more than solely surviving a few years on this physical planet. We have a yearning to do the impossible. *Our hearts were made for You, O Lord, and they are restless until they rest in you. (St. Augustine).*

What dreams do you consider impossible? How attainable would they become if you began believing you could accomplish them? Many of the dreams in our hearts were put there by God even though we don't realize it.

The second story is a Paralympic commercial titled *Samsung - Do What You Can't Human Nature Brand Campaign Commercial 2018*. The video shows a series of "I can't" scenes, from a toddler taking his first steps, to a girl attempting to ride her 2-wheeler without training wheels. Each person's attempt is encouraged with "You can do it." The commercial's scenes switch to "I can't" clips - from a guy playing guitar who "can't play," to a gal welding her bike who "can't get a real job," and finally we watch a young lady learning to take her first steps with an artificial leg. Samsung displays *"We're born to do what can't be done."*

Another ad from Toyota is part of the company's "*Start Your Impossible*" campaign. The ad features Lauren Woolstencroft, born without legs below the knee and no left arm below the elbow. The ad is titled "Good Odds", but that's an oxymoron. The odds were so monumental for this alpine skier from Canada as to be practically impossible. Lauren overcome her handicaps and eventually achieved the feat of becoming an eight-time Paralympic gold medalist.

Have you ever read the children's book The Little Engine That Could? The engine's job was to bring a load of toys up a mountainside to waiting kids. It was difficult for such a small locomotive who could hardly pull herself. Her song "I think I can, I think I can" after the feat was accomplished became "I thought I could, I thought I could."

I always wanted to play the piano proficiently, but I didn't take lessons for long or practice consistently. Is it too late to learn the piano? Another skill I wanted to develop was dribbling a soccer ball deftly. I never learned that skill when I was growing up. Could I learn to dribble proficiently through intentional, consistent practice? Most likely, yes. What "I can't" dreams can you accomplish if you turn your "I can't" into "I can" and act on them?

Video Games

My adult children are avid gamers. A decade ago, they held video game LAN parties where all the guys would bring their game consoles or PCs to play together at one person's house. That was before Internet gaming. Now it's all online. Your team in the game might be scattered all over the U.S. or even in other countries. Language is not even a barrier anymore. As long as you know the rules of the game and recognize who is on your side, you can join. Be careful if you're a newbie. Newbies are often shunned. What makes video games so attractive and addicting? Can you find God while playing these games or are they a "godless" waste of time?

Regardless of the particular game, most video games involve one team battling their opponent. Camaraderie is a key component of the attraction. One of the core needs common to all of us is the need to belong. We all need to belong to a group with a common cause. The members in the group might not be close friends, but being part of the same team still has its benefits.

From the beginning, God created people to be together, not isolated. He put us in families. Families are an important part of growth and maturity. Here is something to ponder::How is playing a video game with teammates like belonging to a family?

Video: Hidden Messages Revealed

Exercises

- List the activities, hobbies, or dreams you wish you could do, but never tried. For instance, "I'd like to try scuba diving, but I can't because…"(then you add an excuse). Maybe the "can't" phrase is what is holding you back. What would it take to make that dream come true?
- Make a list of the videos or games that you like the best.
- Ask yourself "Why?" What is a common theme in these videos and games? What does that say about me? Am I filling a need or are these videos propelling me to take action that will impact those around me in a positive way?

7 Movies: Messages That Influence Your Beliefs

Superhero movies are popular. Often the hero in the movie may not survive until the end -- or he or she may die and come back to life. Most movies have a message that parallels the good news that someone was willing to sacrifice his/her life to save another

It's a Wonderful Life

Who hasn't seen "It's a Wonderful Life"? This movie has a realistic view of life with its power-hungry political figures who do not hesitate to manipulate others to get what they want. Mr. Potter is the powerful rich man in this movie. George Bailey sacrifices a promising career and uses his own savings to help the common folks, the hard-working middle class who struggle to buy their own homes. The moral of the movie is *Your life is valuable. Your impact many others. The world would be different if you had not been born.*

Movies such as this contain obvious messages. Other films require you to dig further to find meaning.

Producers create movies not only to entertain you, but also to persuade you. The visual effects and soundtracks target your emotions to convince you to agree with the producer's viewpoint.

Frozen

"Frozen", one of the highest-grossing movies of all time, was inspired by Hans Christian Andersen's fairy tale "The Snow Queen". The film follows a princess's journey to find her estranged sister, whose magical powers have accidentally encased their kingdom in eternal winter. The movie's climatic theme line is *Only an act of true love can thaw a frozen heart*. Other notable messages in this film include:

> *Fear will be your enemy.*
> *You don't have to live in fear.*
> *True love brings out the best.*
> *Love is putting someone else's needs above your own.*
> *Some people are worth melting for.*

The Dark Knight

"The Dark Knight Rises" features Batman as the superhero and Bane as the enemy. Bane is a terrorist who lives with his fellow evildoers in the sewers. Bane's team steals, kills, and plans to destroy the city with an atom bomb created from a reactor core. Catwoman betrays Batman and leads him into Bane's trap. Bane fights Batman and imprisons him in a well in a remote desert. Batman escapes, and the reactor bomb is activated to explode with no way to stop it -- which will destroy the city. Batman risks his life to haul the bomb away in a helicopter to allow it to blow up outside the city. The helicopter flies over the bay, where it finally explodes. Batman is presumed dead, but later on we learn he escaped. Our superhero saved the city! In other movies such as the Transformer series or Armageddon, the entire world is saved.

The plot of saving the world from evil or destruction may have its roots in the biblical story of redemption. Many films contain a redemption theme as their basis. Often one of the leading characters in the movie will sacrifice his/her life to save the world or to save another person.

You can observe betrayal by Catwoman in the Batman movie above. In a similar way, Judas betrayed his master, Jesus resulting in His death. After He died to save the world, Jesus was in the tomb, dead for three days, but rose to live again.

The Redemption Theme

Many movies portray the protagonist as willing to give his or her life to save someone, including "Five Feet Apart," "Breakthrough," "Saving Private Ryan," "Braveheart," and "Wonder Woman".

Wonder Woman, the heroine who enters the real world from being raised on an female-only island, fights a war to end all wars. She is persuaded that there is evil in all men – i.e., males. One hero in the film sacrifices his life to save the world from destruction. The evil man in this film tries to persuade Wonder Woman to join him to rid the world of men. She is tempted to kill an evil scientist but refuses. She believes love is stronger than evil. When the evil doctor tries to kill her with a laser blast, she deflects the blast onto the enemy and destroys him.

A similar approach to defeating an enemy is demonstrated in "Star Wars: The Rise of Skywalker." As the movie draws to a close, the Emperor turns his lightning force on our heroine, Rey, and she counters it by crossing both of her light sabers to deflect it back on her enemy. The Emperor is destroyed by his own power. The crossed light sabers form a picture of the cross.

In the "Wonder Woman" movie, we hear the idea that all men (males) are evil. Perhaps all of us have missed the mark in some way. The book of Romans states "All have sinned. Not even one is good." Just as the devil tempted Jesus, the heroine, Wonder Woman, was likewise tempted. Wonder Woman a type of savior, is tempted to return evil for evil, taking the easy way out. She passes the test, by refusing to kill. *Love is stronger than death. (Song of Solomon 8:6).* God turns what is meant for evil into good. (See *Gen 50:20*).

In the movie "Kung Fu Panda," an undisciplined Panda named Po, is unexpectedly chosen to fulfill a prophecy and become The Dragon Warrior. Not only would he be the Kung Fu Master, but in this position ne could obtain limitless power by reading from the Dragon Scroll - power that could be used for good or for evil. Po's first mission is to save the Valley of Peace from the evil leopard, Tai Lung who was once in line to be the Dragon Warrior. Po is an unlikely hero, but begins to believe in his true identity as The Dragon Warrior and saves the village by defeating the evil Tai Lung. This is another redemption-themed film.

Each of us longs for a hero to save us. We desire a person to love. We yearn to be acknowledged. We would like to be a hero or heroine to someone else. I believe each of us desires to leave our mark and make a lasting impact on the world.

Do movies reveal your heart motivations?

Movies: Messages That Influence Your Beliefs

What movies grab your heart the most? I like a few types of movies.: Here are the categories and movies for each.

The underdog wins
"Rocky" (1976)
"Rudy" (1993)
"Eddie the Eagle" (2016)
"Miracle" (2004)
"Kung Fu Panda" (2008)
"Facing the Giants" (2006)

Father-son themes: Leadership, Mentorship, Coaching
"I Can Only Imagine" (2018)
"McFarland USA" (2015)
"Field of Dreams" (1989)
"The Lion King" (1994)
"Invictus" (2009)
"Darkest Hour" (2017)

Friendship and Commitment
"The Parent Trap" (1998)
"The Incredibles" (2004)
"The Peanuts Movie" (2015)
"The Fox and the Hound" (1981)
"The Iron Giant" (1999)
"Ratatouille" (2007)

Motivational & Inspirational
"Chariots of Fire" (1981)
"It's a Wonderful Life" (1946)
"Rocky" (1976)
"Remember the Titans" (2000)
"Soul Surfer" (2011)
The Greatest Showman (2017)
"The Blind Side" (2012)

Movies: Messages That Influence Your Beliefs

Exercises

- The next time you watch a movie, take special note of golden nuggets in the dialogue. Dismiss the corny jokes and sift through the superfluous talk and you will glean wisdom. As an exercise at home, watch one of your favorite movies, and write down the nuggets of wisdom that connect with you.
- Make a list of your favorite movies. Categorize them by type as I did above. You will recognize a theme or two that will identify the core values in your heart.
- The next time you watch a movie, take special note of golden nuggets in the dialogue. Dismiss the corny jokes and sift through the superfluous talk and you will glean wisdom. As an exercise at home, watch one of your favorite movies, and write down the nuggets of wisdom that connect with you.
- Make a list of your favorite movies. Categorize them by type as I did above. You will recognize a theme or two that will identify the core values in your heart

SPIRIT EYES

8 Shopping: What's Right in Front of Your Eyes?

Does God leave messages for you in plain sight? If you delve into the not-so-common titles of board games, cereals, and health foods, you will find values beyond what you expected.

You can uncover God's messages to you when shopping. As I mentioned earlier, a preacher on a TV program caught my ear when she mentioned: "First comes the natural, then the spiritual". To me, it meant there was a deeper meaning in the physical world for everything that I only observed on the surface.

I began looking for clues in the natural that had spiritual significance. In the days that followed, I began to see things with new eyes – Spirit Eyes. At Walmart, I bought a bottle of bubbles (wands included). The label read "Miracle Bubbles". That was intriguing. "Miracles" imply a supernatural event. Later that week, I found a couple more products with underlying spiritual meaning. I asked my carpet layer, Joe, "What's the best way to get spots out of a rug?" He replied, "I use Capture

- a spray and powder cleaning agent that draws out the dirt." Always looking for advice, I asked "Do you have a recommendation for furniture polish that would cover scratches? Scrapes mar the surface of this wooden door. What do you recommend?" He raved about the best polish - it covered scratches that no other polish would. Its name? *Liquid Gold*. "What a cool name!", I thought. Let's look at possible spiritual parallels to these items.

What comes to mind when you think of bubbles? I'm speaking of the toy bottles of bubble-making liquid that you might find at a dollar store or toy store. Bubbles are a symbol of fun, freedom, dance, child-like play. Could *Miracle Bubbles* symbolize growing in freedom – expanding our freedom to express ourselves, such as encouraging us to dance and enjoy playful times. It could also make us think about breaking free from past hurts or memories that prevent us from experiencing wholeness.

What about the word "Capture" as in capturing dirt from a carpet? What could dirt represent in a spiritual sense? Sin? Shame? Stuff in our lives that we want to clean up? Perhaps you struggle with bad habits or addictions that you find hard to overcome. Is there a way to capture those irritating issues, get yourself clean so you can start fresh again?

Finally, "Liquid Gold" is used to cover scratches, unsightly blemishes. Gold may symbolize glory, love, God's forgiveness for our messes, a healing balm to soothe our wounds, and to cover our mistakes.

Continue to search beyond the outward appearance. You may not see the same way another person sees. We each perceive uniquely. God will show you the unique way He communicates to you. It will feel exciting and fulfilling.

Shopping: What's Right in Front of Your Eyes?

Cereals and Slogans

Commercials for Trix cereal use the slogan *"Trix is for kids"* to infer that adults are too old or grown-up to enjoy the cereal. When I was a kid, this felt special to me. Consider the Spirit Eyes meaning this slogan could have: Jesus said, "unless you change and become like little children, you will never enter the kingdom of heaven." This is an admonition to us to stop judging and start believing with the imagination and innocence of a child. Taking time to observe simple things such as the title of a cereal box can bring you more insight than you expected!

Another cereal with a long tradition is *Wheaties – The Breakfast of Champions*. The front of the box shows sports figures and other champions, enticing you to buy it. The implication is if you eat this cereal, you will grow muscles, and become strong and athletic like a sports champion.

How about Kellogg's Frosted Flakes? Tony the Tiger has been on this sugary corn flake cereal for decades. His motto is "They're GRRRRRRREAT!". The sound of his cheery voice still rings in my memory.

As you stroll down the cereal aisle, you'll spot ads with pictures on the boxes vying for your attention. I expect kids who watch TV commercials will beg their parents to buy this cereal or that one. Take a second look at the slogans. How can these slogans bring to mind a deeper message?

Healthy Eating

Here are some foods you might encounter in a Health Food Store: Energy products such as

Jym, Reign Total Body Fuel, Cellucor Dynasty Pre-Workout. These energy supplements make it appear you'll get the same results you'd get by going to a gym or working out at a Planet

Fitness place. It doesn't take a lot of imagination to recognize what they're implying.

How about clear skin and beauty aids? *Lumiday® Youth Rejuvenator* and *Radiance Within* sound very inviting, don't they? These two items remind me of a couple of Bible verses. *Isaiah 40:30-31 They that wait upon the Lord shall renew their strength. (KJV)* And for Radiance within *1 Sam 16:7 People look at the outward appearance, but the LORD looks at the heart.(NIV) Proverbs 4:23 Above all else, guard your heart, for everything you do flows from it. (NIV)*

Board Games or Bored Games?

What kind of messages can you find in board games? How important might they be? When you think about something trivial, it implies it's not very important. The game of Trivial Pursuit turns that idea on its head because what it defines as important is the ability to recall a lot of details. Questions revolve around a half-dozen categories such as Sports & Leisure or Arts & Entertainment. The original edition was produced in 1981. Since then, the original questions have become less relevant, so succeeding generations of the game have been produced, including Star Wars editions, 25th-anniversary edition, the Beatles Collection Edition, and others. What an oxymoron "Trivial", that the game became this popular!

The Game of Life by Milton Bradley first appeared in the 1960s but is still popular today in its latest edition (2018). Depending on your age, you'll find it intriguing in different ways. How closely does it relate to reality? It concentrates most on money and least on relationships, except those that increase your value. If you had to create a game of life, what would it look like?

A French film director invented the board game *Risk*. It was originally released in 1957 in France as *The Conquest of the World*, which is an appropriate title. The game has undergone numerous changes over the years, but the objective is still the same: Global Domination. I am familiar with the classic version where you strategize to conquer all the other players and eliminate them one-by-one. It's not much fun for those who have been eliminated. Once players eliminate you, your game time is over until the remaining players finish. I remember the game taking the better part of a day if not two. You had to take chances often or risk losing your armies. What relevance does the game of *Risk* have for us? Let's consider that idea briefly.

Countries over the millennia have attempted to dominate the world. Besides the Roman Empire, there was Alexander the Great and Atilla the Hun. In the past century, Germany attempted to dominate twice, then the Soviet Union. Now we have China, Iran, Iraq, and others in Asia or the Mid-East that are expansionist regimes. with China vying to become a superpower." Islam's goal is to convert everyone to their faith or eliminate the "infidels" who are classified as Western Countries. Christianity at one time used force, i.e. the Crusades in the middle ages, to conquer countries. If you are a believer in Scripture, the law of love and rule of God will eventually fill the earth from sea to sea, also known as the Kingdom of God. I much prefer the "rule" that elevates love, joy, and peace over aggression fighting and war. Love is the currency of the kingdom.

In games such as *Ticket to Ride* and *Catan*, players build railroads or establish settlements. You buy and trade resources to connect your cities or towns. Is that idea similar to *Risk*? In some ways, it is. However, these two games are more team-focused than *Risk*. One point of similarity is they rely on strategy more than chance. The more you plan and practice, the better you get at winning.

Exercises

- Look at the names of products you've bought. What stands out to you? That might contain a hidden message for you. Some examples for you: What are the names of the soap and shampoo you use? Do these have any significance?
- Go through your games to see if there are any that have a message that supports your values.

9 Sports: Pictures Seen 'Round the World'

From events during a Super Bowl to the names of teams and nicknames of players, there are many opportunities to capture messages that speak to you personally.

Every professional sport culminates in championship games to determine the best player or team. The U.S. hosts the Super Bowl for football, the NBA Championship for basketball, the World Series for baseball, the Masters Tournament and PGA Championship for golf, the Stanley Cup Playoffs for hockey, the U.S. Open for tennis, as well as championships for other sports.

Why do we hold these competitions? We long to be recognized for greatness, to be accepted, and even acclaimed by others. Each of us desires to be a champion or expert at something. We yearn to see our team overcome the opponent and become the victor in a contest. Inside each person lies a unique treasure. It wants to be expressed and seen by others. One of the challenges we encounter in encouraging others is to find the gold God has placed inside them and speak out what we see. God can give you the Spirit Eyes to see past the outward appearance to what is not as obvious - the person of the heart and the purpose for which that person was created.

Sports give skilled athletes a chance to "shine." You've seen interviews of athletes who accept both winning and defeat humbly and others who are prideful in their response. Although each of us is responsible for our own decisions and actions, we need others for support, to help us grow in maturity and to point out the treasure inside of us.

We look to sports heroes to be role models. If you examine the person you admire, what qualities do they possess that attract you to him or her? Some might be beauty, handsomeness, poise, skill, precision, running ability, agility, speed, strength, strategy, teamwork, physical prowess, mental toughness, endurance, perseverance, or sacrifice. There are other traits too.

Sports can be categorized into two areas: team sports and individual sports. Some sports that are team sports rely on a single player more than other players. Baseball has a pitcher; football teams rely on the quarterback, and soccer must have a skilled goalie to succeed. Let's examine a couple of sports to draw out potential messages.

Football – What more is there?

The quarterback is the captain of a football team. The ball won't cross into the endzone if the quarterback is mediocre. We can liken the quarterback to the father of a family, the CEO of a company, or the leader of a platoon. Stretch your imagination.

Who can the crowd in a stadium represent? The crowd reminds me of Hebrews 12 which describes the great cloud of witnesses who have gone on before us. They are cheering us to run the race with endurance. Picture God as a quarterback. (A big stretch, right?) We can even find some parallels even here. The quarterback views the entire field. He knows each player's route and whether a wide receives is open or being blocked by an opponent.

In a spiritual sense, God knows the route you're on in life. Can He trust you to take the ball and run the race He's laid out or will you decide on your own path and zigzag without getting to the end zone? He sees the beginning from the end and leads you to a good finish if you keep running and don't give up.

Soccer and basketball are team sports where all players are equally involved. There is no such thing as a one-man team. As a player, you are continually looking for space – a place where there is no opponent near you, so you can receive a pass safely. You must be aware of where each of your teammates is running, so you can advance the ball to the goal or net. Players support each other both on offense and defense, by always looking out for one another. We ought to support each other in life. Look out for one another.

One of the most difficult skills to learn in both soccer and basketball is transitioning from offense to defense at a moment's notice. When you're on the offense, as described above, you spread out so you can receive a pass and move the ball up the field (or down the court). However, once you lose possession of the ball, you must defend your goal or net. You are no longer running into a space, but you switch to either protect your goal or you guard the nearest opponent and pressure him or her to give up the ball.

Is this analogous to your spiritual and emotional life? Do you live continually on the defense, reacting to what you consider are "attacks" from the enemy? Do you live in that fear realm or are you more often at peace? Are you on the offense with spreading a kind word or helping the less fortunate? Perhaps it's time to concentrate on offense. An example of being on the offense is building your spirit up with thankfulness. Thankfulness is good for your physical health as well as your psychological health. This gratitude releases "feel good" chemicals such as endorphins into your bloodstream. Search for "Benefits of Gratitude" online.

In the same way, the right type of music can lift you up vs. create stress. This is another example of being on the offense. Just as gratitude can change your attitude, you can also change your mood by listening to inspirational music. It's fun to be on the offense. Try some of the suggestions in the Exercises section at the end of this chapter.

Sometimes I get edgy when there's too much noise. A sporting event is not the best place to go if you're looking for quiet and peaceful places. Baseball (and golf) are a couple of the most relaxing sports. While attending a baseball game, you can sit and relax with your favorite beverage and your "red hot" hotdog. Baseball is a slow-moving sport, especially compared to basketball.

Playing a game of golf can be a leisurely activity and good exercise if you walk instead of riding in a cart. Watching golf on TV might be more intense than participating yourself, especially if it's a tournament with commentators accentuating every shot. Playing sports is supposed to be fun, but we often make it competitive and add stress instead of enjoying it. When you invest time in physical activities and creative endeavors, you give your logical mind (left brain) a chance to rejuvenate. Your right brain gets energized when playing a sport.

Get your body in motion

Let's consider track and cross-country. *Don't you realize that in a race everyone runs, but only one person gets the prize? So run to win! 1 Cor 9:24 (NLT)*. Most kids love to run. They have endless energy. They love to compete in a race to win. Then they "do it again, but faster!" We view Tour-de-France bicycle marathons. We watch the Indianapolis 500. We attend school events or Park District events, or possibly 5K or 10K races to cheer on our friends or family members. Running the race is an analogy Paul uses to remind us to never give up but keep pushing forward. How often have you felt like giving up? What does it take to keep on running, keep on going in life? A close friend? An encourager? We yearn to be winners, but God has already granted us the biggest prize and it's not a result of performance.

Championship games

Everyone wants to be a winner. We all want to be acknowledged. Championship games abound as I mentioned earlier. Let's take a closer look at a specific championship story, then we'll examine coincidences, predications, and spiritual implications.

In 2013 the Michigan State Spartans football team defeated the Ohio State Buckeyes in the Big Ten Championship game to win their first trip to the Rose Bowl since 1988. It was the 100th Rose Bowl, and Michigan State University would be playing against Stanford.

MSU's previous season, 2012, had been a let down from the 2011 season where they posted an 11-3 record and narrowly lost to Wisconsin in the Big Ten Championship game.

In May of 2013, Spartans Coach Mark Dantonio found himself in Southern California when he decided to drive to Pasadena and drop by the Rose Bowl Stadium. His daughter recorded a video from the field that he showed to the team six months later in December just before that Big Ten Championship game against Ohio State.

"Hey guys, welcome to the Rose Bowl," Dantonio said in the videotaped message. "I had the opportunity to come out here in late May and just walk on the field a little bit, and this is where we make it happen. So, January 1 this year, 2014 as we get into it, it'll be our time. It will be our time. And as I said at the banquet, you will be the ones. "

Dantonio's prediction came true as Michigan State beat previously unbeaten Ohio State 34-24 in that Big Ten Championship game on December 7, 2013.

"I wanted to be there," Dantonio said in an interview months after the Rose Bowl visit in May. "I wanted to walk in there. I wanted to see the field, what it was going to be like to be there."

Coach Dantonio's mantra for 2013 was "Chase it." He told his players, "Dream big!". He declared, "In 50 years, your grandchildren will look up there (at the Rose Bowl list of champions) and be able to see Michigan State again." This is leaving a legacy. It's more than just football and a game. It's preparing for challenges. The reason for "Chase it" or the follow-on mantra of "Chase the moment" is that when you're chasing something, you're moving. We want to be moving toward something, not just staying still and stagnant.

Drawing out the messages behind Michigan's win, let's note the significance of the numbers associated with this historic game.:

- *100th* Rose Bowl,
- *33* years as a coach for Mark Dantonio
- Jersey *#18* as the quarterback Conner Cook.

Number 18 was also worn by other successful quarterbacks such as Peyton Manning. 100 and 33 are particularly noteworthy. *100* can signify completion, fullness as in 100%, or restoration. *33* is double 3's, which may symbolize the 3 dimensions, the Trinity or God. Let's look at messages in some other sports.

Paralympics

Paralympians embody courage and perseverance. As an athlete with a disability, you face the difficulties of adapting to perform in your particular sport. In some cases, this means you must tackle the challenge to learn all over again how to walk or use your injured limb. Think about it. You must push past the ghost pain that often lingers in that limb. You must learn how to dress, take a shower, eat with a new hand, or walk with an artificial leg and foot.

Besides those physical challenges, Paralympians must push beyond what they originally believed was impossible. This effort requires mental toughness. Snowboarders in the downhill events can outperform by far an average person who has all his or her limbs intact.

I expect none of us remember taking our first steps, but we have seen a one-year-old begin the process of letting go of the couch and venturing out on his/her own across the living room carpet. Consider what it would be like to start learning to walk all over again as an adult. You'd have to learn how to balance. You'd look for handrails and walls to grab onto to avoid falling. You would need to learn how to stand up after you've fallen - analogous to learning how to get up after falling when wearing downhill skis. Other muscles would have to take up the slack. So many challenges! The athlete with such a disability has even more obstacles to overcome.

Cheering the underdog on to victory gives us the motivation to keep pressing on. You are in a race – the race of life. *So run to win! 1 Corinthians 9:24.*

Exercises

- List a few of your favorite players and identify what characteristics you see in each of them. Which characters do they have in common?
- List at least 3 of your favorite sports figures and identify the characteristics you see in each of them. Which characteristics are in common among them all? Write them down. Some ideas might be courage, risk-taker, disciplined, well-trained, intelligent. Which of these qualities apply to you? What have you learned about yourself and about the way God made you from this exercise?
- We all are handicapped in some areas. List your top 3 challenges or obstacles. What has been holding you back. What has God told you that you have not completed? Where are you procrastinating? This is a great place to start – the places you have not yet finished.
- In what ways have you been hurt or handicapped emotionally? How is this knowledge useful in growing in maturity?
- After answering the questions above, find a trusted partner to share them with. Make an action plan. Pray together and check your daily, weekly progress. Your plan needs to have baby steps so you can see your incremental progress. A bunch of small steps eventually leads to completing a big step and getting that much closer to your goal.

10 Numbers and Secret Codes

Have you woken up at night to notice your alarm clock displaying 3:33, 12:21, or some other unique combination? Once you learn the meaning of some basic numbers, you will be able to translate God's messages to you.

Messages at McDonald's and Burger King

What if my customer number is not an accident? If God is always communicating (like best friends do), He may be sending me a message through my receipt. Here are examples of my receipts at fast-food restaurants.

I stopped at McDonald's this morning on the way to church. "You're a junk eater!" you might think. No. In reality, I am a healthy eater. McDonald's is our weekly stop on Sundays before church. I anticipate finding another personal message

95

from God at this eating stop. He gives me a message each time I stop at Mc Donald's if I am intentional in using my "Spirit Eyes". It is another place I discover one of his thousands of thoughts toward me. It's another hidden message designed for me to find. I order oatmeal and get a restaurant receipt with God's message to me. What is the hidden message in my receipt? It's encoded in the customer number on the receipt. That number is *mine* – no one else's this morning. It's unique to me – NOT a coincidence. (Remember the belief "There is no such thing as a coincidence"? Nothing God allows is by chance – there is a purpose in everything). God likes to play these games with me.

I take the 3-digits and ask God "What are you speaking to me?" Often, my first thought is to look up those digits in Psalms as a chapter/verse combination. I once got 231, so I look up *Psalm 23:1* which says *"The Lord is my shepherd, I lack nothing"* Is that my message? God is telling me today not to worry about anything because I am complete. With my Father guiding me, I have no lack.

Sometimes I end up in Isaiah or Proverbs or another book in the Bible. If the verse I find talks about God's judgment on Israel, a battle, or something I consider irrelevant, I search somewhere else. Sometimes the number suggests something special from my past. Once I got a receipt with the digits 237. I realized that 237 was the name of the Cub Scout Pack I once attended as a boy. Cub Pack 237 brought back some fond memories. Memories of camaraderie, skits, and Cub Scout den meetings where we often worked on crafts. My mom was the den mother. I reflected on other events such as watching my dad run the pack meeting as the Cub Scout Pack 237 leader. I recognized how God cared for me when I was growing up in providing a nurturing atmosphere where both my parents were involved.

Numbers and Secret Codes

Another time at McDonald's my receipt showed the digits 294. I could not find a verse that was a positive message for me, but I remembered that 294 were the figures that identified the tollway I traveled when I lived in the Chicago area. The 294 Tollway reminded me of my college days and vacation times. I lived in that suburban area from high school days through college and beyond. Some messages are simply for me to enjoy and not wrangle over decoding.

I realize not everyone loves math but we're not attempting to solve an algebra problem or use calculus to resolve an integral. You can find adventure in discovering messages in numbers by appreciating fun numerical combinations. Your phone number, address, and Social Security Number are all unique numerical characters that are used to identify you.

Besides the unique digits we encounter in our lives, numbers are important in Scripture as well as in our lives. One in every five scriptural verses contains a number. The meaning of these frequently used numerals reveals the mind of God toward us.

The interpretation of numbers in the Bible (Biblical numerology) is quite different from the way numbers are interpreted by secular means (secular numerology. Some numbers are particularly important. The number five represents grace. When I see triples or double numbers, I get enthralled. I sense it's a hidden message from God. Four means God's created works. Seven is completeness. 40 means testing, trials. See the resources at the end of this chapter for more information.

I started noticing God's hidden messages in my Burger King customer numbers on my receipt. I held on to those receipts for a time. When I get a number such as 271, I am challenged to interpret its meaning. I might first search for a scriptural counterpart such as a verse in the Bible, for example, Psalm 27:1 or Isaiah 27:1. At other times, the figure is significant in a different way. 34 was my student ID in grammar school. We wrote those digits in front of our name on every paper we turned in. (Giving every student a number helped the teacher alphabetize the 53 papers in our class when she recorded our grades). I liked 34. It was also my jersey number on the basketball team years later in high school. I felt that God was reminding me of good memories I experienced as a child. He knows my name AND my number.

Here are meanings for the first 12 numerals derived from studying their use in the Bible. I use these as a code translator when I'm on my way, whether I'm shopping or doing errands. You can find references to the meaning of these numbers from people who have researched numbers in the Bible or by searching "Biblical meaning of numbers".

- 1=God or unity
- 2= double
- 3=Godhead (Triune God)
- 4= door
- 5=grace
- 6=man
- 7=completion
- 8=new beginnings
- 9=judgment
- 10=journey/wilderness
- 11=transition
- 12=government.

Using the above translator, can you create a message from your address? If that 3459 address on your mailbox is not just a random number, what might it mean? You can decipher the address above as the Door of God's Grace. To apply that to my life means I can give others the benefit of the doubt, or release grace. When I succeed in doing that, I leave any judgment to God, who is far more fair than I am. My responsibility is to be a Grace Giver.

Numbers and Secret Codes

I glance at my odometer from time to time and it produces some enjoyable combinations, such as the palindrome 113311. A palindrome is a number that reads the same forwards or backwards. Sometimes the odometer contains the same digits as my trip meter. In the example above my trip meter might read 13.3 resulting in a bunch of 3's for me to enjoy. I like 3's – symbolic of God.

Have you translated the characters on your license plate? This is an entertaining activity, especially if you have a random series of symbols combining letters and digits. You may be asked for your license number when filling out an application, or parking temporarily for a blood donation. I invent a phrase from the letters on my plate. Then I take the numbers and hunt for a verse. Assume my letters were HGL. You can translate this into "Here God Lives". It is heartening to remember God is with us (Immanuel). Let's say the digits on my plate are 429. After some exploring, I find *Isaiah 42:9 which reads See, the former things have taken place, and new things I declare; before they spring into being, I announce them to you. (NIV)* It may take some trial and error before you find a verse or meaning for the numbers, but don't give up. The more you practice the easier it will get.

I've mentioned several ways I began enjoying numbers more when I discovered God could speak to me through them. Give it a try the next time you're at a fast-food restaurant and you're given a receipt.

You can become quite analytical when "looking deeper" into the everyday occurrences, yet you still must remain curious enough to let your imagination flow without judging. Your divinely inspired imagination is what I call "Spirit Eyes" when you're guided by the Holy Spirit.

One place where our imagination runs wild is in the nighttime world of dreams. In the next chapter, we'll explore the realm of dreams and learn that they come from various sources, not all of them internal.

Exercises

Use the meaning for each number from 1 to 12 from this chapter for the following.
- What might God's message to you be from your license plate? If you have a combination of letters and digits, create a phrase using the letter as an acronym.
- The next time you get a receipt from a fast-food restaurant, look for meaning in your customer number.
- Decipher the meaning in the address of your house.
- When numbers attract your attention, make time to investigate why.

References:
http://www.abbalovesus.com/Numbers.html
https://reasonsforhopejesus.com/the-meaning-of-numbers-in-the-bible/

SPIRIT EYES

11 Dream Language: Where the Spirit Reveals

Dreams are called night parables. Jesus often told stories in parable form. At night, your spirit is open to thoughts and mental images from God. With your body at rest and your brain disengaged from active thought, it's a perfect time for your spiritual Companion to slip you a message. You can unpack the picture language of dreams when you partner with the Spirit and practice thinking symbolically.

I don't dream," you might say. Or, maybe you're one of the many who would agree with the statement "I know I dream. I just don't remember my dreams after I wake up." Neuroscience has shown that everyone dreams, but not everyone remembers their dreams. Dreaming is necessary for our brain to recycle and refresh itself every day.

Ever since I started paying more attention to my dreams, I remember more of them. What helps is writing them down as soon as I wake up, otherwise, they quickly evaporate. I have a lot of dreams that are common to many people: dreams of losing teeth, being chased, being unable to find my home, etc.

Have you had dreams of being chased? Of losing teeth, of falling, flying, driving, or diving? These are among the most common types of dreams.

Where do dreams come from?

Before we delve into how God can give us messages through our dreams, let's look at the sources of dreams. There are various ways to describe these, but I like Cindy McGill's idea from her book, "What Your Dreams Are Telling You." Cindy describes dreams as coming from 3 sources:
1. Truth (God)
2. Yourself (your subconscious)
3. A lie (evil spirits)

The idea of three sources is in contrast to the secular viewpoint that claims all dreams come from your inner psyche. Pay attention to your dreams and take time to unpack them. You will discover meaning and possibly find direction that will help you in your life's journey. Applying the meaning of the dream to your life will enrich your growth into becoming the person you were created to be.

Let's examine each of the three sources of dreams.

A dream that comes from God is often filled with brilliant color, good feelings, hopeful outcomes. In this dream you may also sense peace and a warm sense of contentment. This type of dream is life-giving, encouraging.

The second kind of dream comes from yourself. This type is the most common. For example, I often dream about being chased and hiding from the bad guys. It's as if I'm in a foreign country and the evil army is coming after me. I try to hide and hope they won't find me. It's unsettling with muted colors. In other dreams I find myself at a conference in a hotel. Often, I cannot get back to my hotel room, or I try to get there another way and cannot find the right stairway.

Before I could drive, I would dream I was in the passenger seat in the car and my door would fly open. I was afraid I would fall out of the car. Sometimes I would have to take over driving the car. It was like something you would see in an old TV program where the driver of a semitrailer (a dad) became unconscious, and the 10-year-old son had to grab the steering wheel, but could not brake because his dad's foot was stuck on the accelerator.

The third type of dream is scary or nightmarish. This dream is usually dark in tone as well as fearful, or it can evoke other negative emotions. It can come from your own fears or from the influence of evil spirits. This dream needs to be discarded or flipped in meaning. It can be changed to a positive meaning by flipping the dream to its opposite intent.

You might say "I never dream in brilliant colors or get God-dreams. Even if many of your dreams do not come from God, God can still speak to you through any kind of dream. I will give you some examples of how you can learn from dreams that originate from yourself. Then, I will elaborate a bit more on how to interpret your dreams to get the core meaning from them.

When I analyze a dream of mine, I find it's often a compilation of things I've seen or experienced very recently. It could be a combination of a TV show I just watched the night before plus a class I attended. It could be something I'm hoping for. For example, the other night I dreamt that our kitchen table was completely clear of all paper. In the dream I wondered "Did my wife put those piles of papers somewhere?" That was the dream. When I went to the table for breakfast the morning after, I saw the table just as it had been left the night before, with the two piles of papers there. That scene jogged my memory back to the dream. One interpretation of this dream is that I yearn to control my environment and keep things in order. I want to see my desk clear, clean tables and dresser tops. It's a battle I have yet to win.

What is the application of this dream interpretation – of wanting order in your life, but unable to bring it into reality? First, I can recognize that as a need. Your brain works harder when it has to sift through piles of papers, lists of emails, and toolboxes full of tools to find the one item you're looking for. Simplifying my life by eliminating all the extras, including too many T-shirts, would be freeing. What is the application for me? I can make a plan to move in the direction of getting rid of stuff. Regardless of the specific steps to that goal, the action of getting rid of excess papers would free me from stress. Getting rid of stuff will allow me to invest my time where it counts the most.

God is not complex in the way he communicates with us. Dreams are a picture language he uses to communicate – often without words. He speaks to us in our unique way. However, we need to learn the language of dreams in order to extract the true meaning and not misinterpret them.

The Language of Dreams

Dream interpretation requires two skills. The first skill is the ability to think symbolically. The second skill we need is the ability to connect with the Giver of dreams.

Dream language is symbolic. This is not where we live in our waking moments. For the most part, we explain the world around us logically. Business people, engineers, and architects, for example, think logically. Artists, musicians, crafters, and designers are more apt to think more creatively, symbolically, and with more imagination. We must learn this imaginative type of thinking to properly interpret dreams.

Why not just get a symbol dictionary? A symbol dictionary is not the final authority on uncovering the meaning. Two people can have a very similar dream, but it will have a different interpretation based on the individual's experiences and makeup. For example, Jon has a dream of a dog that is following him. Jon loves dogs. This dream is positive to him because he agrees with the slogan "A dog is man's best friend". Sherry, however, has had negative experiences with dogs, having been afraid of them as a child. A dog following her is more reminiscent of a dog chasing her. She sees dogs as aggressive, mean-spirited. This dream has a negative feeling for her. Another question we could ask is "What kind of dog was it?" A pit bull has a different personality than a poodle.

Dream Interpretation is another place where we need God's help. If we expect God to speak to us in our dreams, we must allow Him to show us how to interpret them as well. We need a partner to help interpret dreams and I call that partner "Holy Spirit". I also like to work in teams, because each person has a unique view of the dream, even after going through dream interpretation training.

God has chosen to communicate with us through dreams and visions, *your young men will see visions, your old men will dream dreams. (Acts 2:17).* God declares that He will counsel us at night through our dreams. *I will bless the Lord who has counseled me. Indeed, my mind (inner man) instructs me in the night (Ps. 16:7 NASB).*

God guides us and warns us through our dreams, calling us to change as it mentions in Job chapter 33. We spend one-third of our lives asleep. That's a huge portion of our lives. It's a time when we're most vulnerable and open to hearing God's messages to us. As Job 33 talks about, we can receive instruction then that could save us from harm in our lives.

Tips for interpreting dreams

Tip 1: Start a dream journal.

Keep a journal or notebook and pen next to your bed to record your dreams. In lieu of a written record, you can record your dreams on your phone using the voice recorder app. Then, transcribe them the next day. You might use the speech-to-text capability in a note program such as Google Keep or Evernote or even an email. As soon as practical, print out the dream and process it.

Tip 2: Layout the dream.

Diagram the dream. You can just throw the major points randomly on paper and then circle the three or four main points. An alternative method is to sketch the dream. Be creative in how you do this. The creative side of your brain is key in interpreting a dream.

Tip 3: Find the focal point of the dream.

Locate the focal point or central character. You can ask "If this were object or person were left out of the dream, would it still make sense?" This step takes practice. Often someone else can see it better than the dreamer.

Tip 4: Translate each main point into its symbolic meaning.

Using a different color pen or marker, write the symbolic meaning of each major point above it. Be aware that dreams about people you know are rarely about them, but rather what they represent in your life. A boss, for example could represent your relationship to authority.

A fork in the road could mean "decision time". A kitchen often represents a place of preparation. A car takes you "where you're going in life". A house is "Where you live". Depending on the context, the meaning will change.

Tip 5: Create a story from the symbolic meaning.

Looking at only the meanings of the symbols (colored ink), combine them into a short paragraph for the interpretation. Pay attention to the tone and the context before you interpret your symbols.

Avoid the temptation to describe the objects in the dream. Pretend you only know the symbolic meaning. You might re-write those colored-pen items on a separate sheet to help with this. Here is where engaging with Holy Spirit is vital. Constantly ask Holy Spirit for help as you lay out the objects on paper or whiteboard. Practice recognizing His whisper, which might come to you as random thoughts.

For further details on how to interpret your dreams search for Adventures in Daily Living course coming later this year titled *Hearing God Through Dreams*.

Exercises

- What dreams have you had that recur? Processing these will tell you something about what's going on in your life. Once you resolve that issue, this dream will stop recurring.
- Have you dreamt in vivid color? These dreams may be from heaven – the first type. Journal your feelings and what you feel God was telling you.
- What is your most troubling dream? Does the theme behind this dream seem to repeat often? What in your life may be causing this? Keep journaling and praying and you will get insight into the reason.

12 Go Exploring

I've only scratched the surface in ways that God may be leaving personal messages for you. How many more ways could you add to this book? Discover the unique ways God communicates with you. Let your God-inspired imagination run loose.

END NOTES

Art: Can a Painting Leave You Breathless?

Hyun, Janet. *Victory - Art Prints.*
https://www.janethyun.com/store/p366/horse.html
Used with permission

Lipov, Felix. *Lobby in the Rookery Building, a historic land mark located at 209 South LaSalle Street in the Loop community area of Chicago in Cook County, Illinois. 2015.*
https://www.123rf.com . Standard License

Hitzeman, Kat. *Miriam. Beauty for Ashes.*
http://kaleidoscopeeyestosee.weebly.com/gallery.html
Used with permission.

Book Cover courtesy of Klopacka, Jozef. *Goddess eye and Color space background with stars.*
https://www.123rf.com . Standard License

SPIRIT EYES

ABOUT THE AUTHOR

Dan Lacine facilitates the Prophetic Ministry at Destiny Church in Rochester. Prophetic in the sense of hearing God – sensing the ways he speaks to us. Dan has been involved in prophetic ministry for over 20 years. He teaches classes in person and online on Growing in the Prophetic, Immanuel Journaling, and Spirit-led Dream Interpretation. He inspires people to look for opportunities every day to share God's encouraging words with people they encounter.

SPIRIT EYES

www.ingramcontent.com/pod-product-compliance
Lightning Source LLC
Chambersburg PA
CBHW072204100526
44589CB00015B/2365